DATE DUE

FEB 2 1970

DEC 21 1970

Top Management Development and Succession

Top Management Development and Succession

An exploratory study

by

Albert S. Glickman

Clifford P. Hahn

Edwin A. Fleishman

Brent Baxter

of

AMERICAN INSTITUTES FOR RESEARCH in the Behavioral science
Washington, D.C.

November 1968

SUPPLEMENTARY PAPER NO. 27 *issued by the*

COMMITTEE FOR ECONOMIC DEVELOPMENT

A CED Supplementary Paper

This Supplementary Paper is issued by the Business-Education Committee of the Committee for Economic Development in conformity with the CED Bylaws (Art. VII, Sec. 6) which authorize the publication of a manuscript as a Supplementary Paper if:

a) It is recommended for publication by the Project Director of a subcommittee because in his opinion, it "constitutes an important contribution to the understanding of a problem on which research has been initiated by the Business-Education Committee" and,

b) It is approved for publication by a majority of an Editorial Board on the ground that it presents "an analysis which is a significant contribution to the understanding of the problem in question."

This Supplementary Paper relates to the Statement on National Policy, *Educating Tomorrow's Managers*, issued by the CED Research and Policy Committee in October 1964.

The members of the Editorial Board authorizing publication of this Supplementary Paper were:

This paper has also been read by the Business-Education Advisory Board and the Research Advisory Board, the members of which under the CED Bylaws may submit memoranda of comment, reservation, or dissent.

While publication of this Supplementary Paper is authorized by CED's Bylaws, except as noted above its contents have not been approved, disapproved, or acted upon by the Committee for Economic Development, the Board of Trustees, the Research and Policy Committee, the Business-Education Committee, the Business-Education Advisory Board, the Research Staff, or any member of any board or committee, or any officer of the Committee for Economic Development.

Foreword

Rapid social and technological changes will continue to impose new demands on American business management. Given the profound impact of the American corporation on all aspects of our national life, the quality of management becomes a factor of increasingly vital concern to our society. The decisions of corporate management not only affect directly the future of American industry but also influence the role of the United States in world affairs.

An awareness of the need for finding ways to improve the education of business managers led the Committee for Economic Development, through its Business-Education Committee, to study the problems involved and issue a Statement on National Policy on this subject in October 1964. The statement, *Educating Tomorrow's Managers,* focused on the formal educational objectives, methods, and content of the business schools. But it recognized that beyond this, "greater efforts must be made to solve the critical problem of how to develop managerial ability and the quality of leadership."

Pursuing this line of thought, the Business-Education Committee began an exploration of top management development and succession in the American corporation. Over a period of two years, the Committee reviewed and discussed a considerable body of literature on this subject, including studies based on the extensive experience of management consultants, the findings of the behavioral sciences, and analyses of university-sponsored programs. From this discussion emerged a consensus on the following broad positions:

1. A great deal of what appears regarding management development in books, company programs, and university-sponsored and other outside programs can be classified as "conventional wisdom" and appears to be inappropriate as a practical guide for top management.

2. There is a wealth of pious statements in the literature about what companies are doing, based on what they *think* they are doing. But there is often a disparity between this and what is actually being done.

3. Many companies appear to think of management development as something that is done to the individual rather than as a step in a continuous and integrated management process, involving not only the motives and development of the individual but likewise the philosophy, objectives, and organizational structure of the corporation. The interplay between individual development and the particular corporate environment in which this takes place requires close study of the *total* corporate setting; to study only the formal education program of a corporation hardly suffices.

4. The corporate environment, which embodies the formal authority system, policies and practices, the control system, and the wages and jobs set by organization structure, is created by top management. Hence, development must begin at the very top, and if change is needed, that must also occur at the top. The leadership of business must think more about what it is doing and why, and there must be a willingness to apply rigorous self-examination.

The lack of solid and substantial knowledge about the management process deeply concerned the members of the Business-Education Committee. The implications were at once both disturbing and ironic. Here, in the country regarded by the rest of the world as the model for the development of modern management, the experts in the field could find in the main not a consistent body of theory and practice but rather a combination of intuition and piecemeal knowledge that indeed is often contradictory.

It was agreed that basic research must be undertaken to develop a solid body of knowledge in this field. Though the Business-Education Committee recognized that CED is not suited to such an enterprise, it was felt that something useful might be accomplished through a pilot study that would yield information on the current practices of American corporations in management development and succession. This in turn might suggest leads for further research. In this undertaking, the Business-Education Committee was able to secure the cooperation of trustee corporations that have achieved effectiveness in enhancing management performance through their development and succession policies.

To implement this the Committee for Economic Development commissioned the American Institutes for Research, a research organization with expertise in this field, to conduct "An Exploratory Study on Top Management Development and Succession." It should be borne in mind that this was intended as an *exploratory* study only. As it is based on discussions with executives in thirteen corporations affiliated with CED, the sample is neither comprehensive nor representative, although it does cover diverse fields, including banking, retailing, manufacturing, and public utilities in various parts of the country. The people interviewed were those who had been recently promoted to top management positions as well as those who participated in the promotion decisions. The purpose of the study was to get insights into how top management development decisions are made in a few relatively large and well-managed corporations.

As the subject is of such tremendous concern and interest to management and as the report tends to raise questions that provoke self-analysis, the trustee members of the Business-Education Committee recommended that it be published for wider distribution as a CED Supplementary Paper. Further, as the report is a careful and realistic description of how people do get selected for top management, based on the practice of thirteen large corporations that have been relatively successful in management development, the research advisors of the Business-Education Committee recommended that it be published for use by university groups, by students of business and management, and by top management to stimulate their thought and perhaps further research.

In light of the discussions by the members and advisors of the Business-Education Committee, four findings in the report are of particular interest: 1] Development and succession of top management is not simply an extension of the process that operates at the lower levels of management; 2] selection for the top ranks of a large corporation depends on being identified at an early stage in one's career and remaining continuously visible to those who select their successors; 3] the selection of executives is a process that extends over a long period of time; and 4] there is practically no solid information available to evaluate the methods of top management development and succession.

It is this last finding that has led the authors of the report to recommend in the final section a plan for a comprehensive research program. They cite some fifteen studies that could be undertaken for "systematic research in operational contexts of sufficient scope, with adequate control over sufficient time and within a consistent conceptional framework, to provide reliable, practically meaningful findings that are translatable into effective management decisions and courses of action."

There are several aspects of this research plan that should command the attention of all students of management, whether within corporations or on the outside. It is recognized that management development will continue to be an art rather than a science or an applied technology. There is a stress on the need for research into the differences among individuals, groups, and organizations, as well as the need for studying changes and interactions among these entities over a period of time. It is suggested that statistical comparisons should be based on representative samples, including not only those who do succeed in moving to the top but also those who do not. It is not contemplated that a single major comprehensive research program into management development and succession be undertaken. Rather, the research plan provides a consistent framework whereby a great variety of research questions can be profitably examined.

I emphasize these points in light of the discussions by the trustee members of the Business-Education Committee. It is their belief that top executives of large American corporations, employing the means presently available, generally do an effective job in selecting people for advancement on the basis of personal characteristics, potentials, educational backgrounds, and other intangibles. Top management follows performance over a long period of time in a gradual step-by-step process that involves the continuous evaluation of a man and his career. Because this process does involve intangibles, it cannot be fully reduced to paper. However, it is the group's general feeling that corporate top management should be stimulated to attempt more organized and precise evaluation of this process within their own companies and to exchange their experience with other companies. Until American corporations more generally have engaged in such systematic research, evaluation, and planning in regard to management development and succession, a meaningful comprehensive research program in this area probably will not be possible. It is to be hoped that this Supplementary Paper will stimulate such efforts by individual companies. Also, Donald C. Stone, in his comments* on this paper, points out the applicability of the report's proposals to the management development processes of governments and of educational institutions, which have lagged far behind the better-managed business corporations in providing executive leadership.

In behalf of CED, I would like to extend thanks to all those who cooperated in this two-year study project of the Business-Education Committee. A particular obligation is owed to those CED trustees and the executives of their companies participating in the pilot research study. Another debt of gratitude is owed to the research advisors who worked with the Committee. Finally, I

* See Memorandum by Donald C. Stone, Member, CED Research Advisory Board, page 80.

would like to express appreciation to the authors of this report, who directed the pilot study conducted by the American Institutes for Research, and to Lawrence R. Kegan, CED Director of Special Studies, who acted as Project Director throughout the Business-Education Committee's effort to shed light on the subject of management succession and development.

John F. Merriam
CHAIRMAN
BUSINESS-EDUCATION COMMITTEE
COMMITTEE FOR ECONOMIC DEVELOPMENT

AUTHORS' ACKNOWLEDGMENTS

The Business-Education Committee of the Committee for Economic Development and its research advisors played an active role in encouraging this study, formulating the approach, and clearing the way for its implementation. In all of these activities, as well as at various stages in carrying out the study and preparing this report, Lawrence R. Kegan, Project Director of the CED Subcommittee on Management Development and Succession in Business and Director of Special Studies for CED, was of great help. The authors are especially indebted to the executives who volunteered the participation of their companies, to their staffs who furnished information and facilitated arrangements of interviews, and certainly not least of all to the interviewees who responded so fully and candidly.

Contents

Foreword   vii
1. Introduction and Summary   1
2. Factors Affecting Top Management
   Development and Selection   12
3. Factors Affecting the "Take-Off" to Top Management   34
4. Educational and Organizational Factors
   in Development   47
5. Plan for a Research Program   66
   Outline of Topics Covered in Interviews   76
Index   83

1

Introduction and Summary

The Aims and Objectives

Every large corporation has developed a careful and elaborate plan for allocation of its capital resources. Through the system of annual and long-range budgeting, management gives direction and exercises control of organizational components to optimize the effectiveness of the corporate whole. Extensive records are maintained by corporations so that an evaluation can be made about the effectiveness with which policy has been formulated and operations carried out. The details of such systems may be at issue among managers, but their fundamental need is unquestioned.

However, in the case of *human* resources, systematic analysis, procedure, and evaluation are not accorded the same universal acceptance as essential elements of corporate policy. Unfortunately, the *people* who make the decisions that determine how well or poorly capital is used are treated much like an unknown variable in the equation for corporate success.

Yet among American business leaders the conviction is strongly voiced that the rising generation holds the key to the future of American industry, and indeed to the position of the United States in world affairs. Of vital concern to business leaders are the questions: "Where is top management to come from?" "How are tomorrow's corporate leaders to be prepared for those responsibilities?"

1

In 1961, Dr. Edgar H. Schein said, "The continuing rash of articles on the subject of developing better managers suggests, on the one hand, a continuing concern that existing methods are not providing the talent which is needed at the higher levels of industry and, on the other hand, that we continue to lack clear-cut formulations about the process by which such development occurs."[1] The rash of articles has continued and the concerns have not diminished.[2]

Preparation for Business Leadership,[3] a 1964 report of research sponsored by the Committee for Economic Development (CED), dealt with the question of what is the best preparation for business leadership and gave particular attention to the programs in university schools of business. Among the implications drawn from attitudes and opinions expressed in interviews by sixty-six chief executive officers of leading American corporations the following are most relevant here:[4]

> Formal education will be less important to total experience and continuing development as a man approaches the age when top management leadership is in sight.
>
> Industry must assume the major burden for both developing and making effective use of mature executives.

In meeting the challenge of understanding the making of the modern executive, the CED Business-Education Committee sought to probe beyond the confines of conventional management wisdom. It commissioned the American Institutes for Research (AIR) to explore further into the field of management development.

---

[1] E. H. Schein, "Management Development as a Process of Influence," *Industrial Management Review*, II (May 1961), p. 59–77.

[2] A most comprehensive relevant review has recently been completed by M. D. Dunnette, J. P. Campbell, E. E. Lawler, and K. E. Weick, sponsored by the Richardson Foundation. It can serve as a report on the state of the art, with which we will not burden this report. It is to be published in 1969 by McGraw-Hill under the title *Management Effectiveness*.

[3] F. A. Bond, D. A. Leabo, and A. W. Swinyard, *Preparation for Business Leadership: Views of Top Executives*, Michigan Business Reports No. 43, Bureau of Business Research, Graduate School of Business Administration, University of Michigan, Ann Arbor, 1964.

[4] *Ibid.*, p. 48.

The object of this study was to learn more about the factors affecting advancement to top management positions by analyzing what takes place when decisions on management succession are being made. Specifically, it sought to shed more light upon how progress toward senior executive status is influenced by factors such as management development activities, organization policies, supervisory practices, personal characteristics, experience, and background.

The plan of attack was worked out in several working sessions with members of the CED Business-Education Committee and its advisors. The subjects of the study were people who had recently succeeded to high management positions. We asked them how, as they saw it, they had reached these positions. The people who chose them were asked what facts and factors entered into their decision-making process. We wanted to deal with events and decisions while they were still sharp in the minds of the people to whom we spoke. This was not to be a consumer survey of likes and dislikes regarding education, training and development policies, procedures, or courses.

We tried to avoid an artificial situation that would oblige interviewees to act like experts on education, training, and development. It was not assumed that their experience, background, or status automatically qualified them for that role. It was taken for granted that this was a select group of successful American businessmen who could tell how they themselves had acted and reacted in situations involving their own and others' career development.

In conducting our interviews with the individuals who had been promoted and those who had chosen them, we used a common point of departure and a frame of reference that was consistent without being unduly constricting. We started interviews by asking for information about the recent promotion. Then we worked back to uncover what elements had been important in determining the final promotion choice. The interviewers put constant emphasis on what the individuals directly involved did or what happened to them, and what *they* considered to be important in their experience, judgments, and decisions.

The Executive Level Studied

The study was conducted in thirteen CED-affiliated corporations engaged in diverse aspects of banking, retailing, manufacturing, and public utilities. Their officers, who were CED trustees, volunteered their companies' participation. Clearly, such a small group of corporations cannot be regarded as a representative sample. However, within the limits imposed by affiliation with CED and by the necessity to keep the number small, the intention was to include companies with as widely varied characteristics as possible in organizational structure, geographic dispersion, size, type of business, development program, management philosophy, growth rate, and so on.

In preliminary contacts with each of these corporations, background was obtained on the management development program, the decision-making process in executive succession, what personnel information was available and how it was used. Vita for prospective interviewees was also obtained.

After joint consideration by AIR, and company representatives, several recently promoted executives (within the past year and one-half in most cases) were chosen as subjects. Though no hard and fast definitions were established, preference was given to general managers rather than technical or functional specialists. Decision-makers who were influential in these promotions were identified. Schedules of interviews with the promotees and decision-makers were then arranged. Table 1 categorizes positions held by the promotees and decision-makers.

Although the total number of promotees and decision-makers came to about the same number, the ratios varied by company. Thus, in one company a single decision-maker might report on three promotees, in another case three decision-makers might talk about a single promotee, in other instances a different decision-maker would be interviewed concerning each promotee interviewed, and in one instance, a promotee also reported as a decision-maker in the case of another subordinate. As originally scheduled, at least one decision-maker was to be interviewed for each promotee interviewed. In a few cases the exigencies of pressing business coincided with the scheduled interview, so that an interview took place with either a promotee or a decision-maker rather than both, or with a last-minute substitution of a proxy close to the decision-maker.

Those who served as liaison for companies or were part of the personnel or management development staffs were not tabulated below. They, too, provided essential information about how their development processes operated and, in some instances, supplemental information on promotees, decision-makers, and organizational structure and climate.

The feasibility of this study's approach—the involvement of top management in sanctioning and planning the project—has been amply demonstrated. Cooperation was not a problem. Once they fully understood the interviewers' purpose, most participants entered into the spirit of the endeavor without apparent reservation. Their responses were generally open and candid, and very little prodding was necessary. Their eagerness to see the study results was expressed frequently. The fact that senior officers from their own companies had been personally involved in the development of this study, that

Table 1. Distribution of Interviewees

Current Position	NUMBER OF INTERVIEWS		
	Promotees	Decision-Makers	Total
Chairman or vice-chairman		5	5
Director		1	1
President	2	8	10
Vice-president	20	18	38*
Assistant to president		1	1
General manager	2	2	4
Sales manager	2		2
Merchandising manager	1		1
Head of organization units	8		8
Personnel development director		1	1
Total	35	36	71

* One vice-president was interviewed both as a promotee and as a decision-maker.

they had made a voluntary commitment to have their companies cooperate and were, in most instances, directly participating in interviews themselves, quite naturally had a salutary effect upon the motivation of all concerned.

The Method

As previously indicated, the strategy of interviewing was not to ask about programs or about the positions people thought they ought to hold, but to talk in real-life terms about the careers of these men and how they got where they are today.

An open-end conversational format was employed, lasting in most cases between one and two hours. The participants were given assurances of anonymity. The interviewers, who were four senior members of the AIR staff,[5] used the outline of topics found at the end of Chapter 5 to guide content coverage. No strict order or structure was followed, however. The only restraint imposed upon the discussion of these topics was relevance to the major issues. Most typical was an approach to the promotee in these terms: "As you see it, how did you come to occupy your present position?" To a decision-maker a typical opening might be: "How was the decision arrived at to select Mr. P. for his present job?"

The interviewees were asked to respond in their own words and manner. Follow-up questions were inserted to extend coverage, bring out specific information and experience, and achieve clarification. The contents of the interviews were subsequently analyzed by the interviewers to extract the questions, concepts, and principles that seemed to be expressed. Each interviewer first derived his hypotheses from attacking the data contained in his own interviews. Then, the interviewers worked together to cross-check, cross-fertilize, and refine the emerging rational products.

[5] Dr. Brent Baxter, Vice-President and Director of Research; Dr. Edwin A. Fleishman, Vice-President and Director of the Washington office; Dr. Albert S. Glickman, Director, Institute for Research on Organizational Behavior; and Mr. Clifford P. Hahn, Director, Human Resources Research Program.

The Perspective

This is an *exploratory* study. The number of companies involved is small. The typical company under scrutiny is relatively large and successful and it takes an active interest in management development. The people and companies included constitute a select, not a representative, group. The promotees we spoke to and about were the "chosen people." Less attention has been given to the people who have not yet "made it." The approach has been more intensive than extensive in order to make the most of the limited time and cases available.

Our ambitions here do not extend to discovery of *the* answers to problems of management development and succession. Our aspirations are modest: to formulate some tentative hypotheses and principles and to generate some concepts, ideas, and insights that may point the way toward better answers. We seek to be provocative rather than definitive: to confront those responsible for shaping future management development decisions and programs with challenges to stereotyped thinking. We hope that this report will stimulate others to take a fresh look at structure, policy, procedures, and decision-making of their own business, industry, or organization, and that it will help them to construct programs to meet the particular needs of their organizations. This study is not intended to offer prescriptive guidelines for management development or a model to be copied.

We offer these cautions and then plunge forward, so that having once pointed out pitfalls we may hereafter reduce tedious repetition of qualifying phrases surrounding the findings and interpretations. We trust the reader to temper what follows with the realism of his own experience.

At the outset, let us specify the angle from which we are looking at the management development process. We are not greatly concerned here with the management masses in the midrange, but with the few who get to the top. The main question here is, What sets the senior level "successors" and the decisions affecting them apart from the rest? Is it personnel attributes? Training? Experience? Supervision? Organizational policy, structure, or climate? What else?

Most descriptions of management development systems come from their builders; the personnel and training experts. They usually look at the system broadside, superimposing organization chart upon corporate structure. They then describe the cross-sectional view at each rung of the career ladder where administrative and training procedures are instrumented to move people through channels.

That is *not* the way we are doing it. We are looking at it through the eyes of our interviewees in the executive suite. To use a naval analogy, we are looking down from the captain's bridge. From here, the profile of the ship looks very different than it does from sea level. Heretofore, little data about management development has been collected from this vantage point.

We may expect that to the men in command—the "captains of industry" who make the key decisions—the people close at hand are prominent and highly visible. Those below are less distinct and to varying degrees obscured from view and attention. In defining and evaluating the development and succession system, we might therefore expect them to correlate the effectiveness of the system with their estimates of the adequacy of the personnel it brings to the top.

It should also be taken into account that this is a retrospective history provided by people who are a product of their particular generation. Their experiences in the world and in their enterprise cannot be expected to be duplicated in the backgrounds of future executives. In other words, the adult life experience of most of those in senior management positions today embraces both the Great Depression and World War II. To a man of thirty these are relatively remote historical episodes. Hence, it is safe to assume that in and out of the business world the differences between these generations would lead to differences in value systems, motivations, and interpretations of experience. They also impose problems of communication.

Another factor that colors this material is that most of the companies that we dealt with had rather well-established and formalized management development programs. That is, their policy depended primarily upon inside recruitment or selection to fill positions at the level of general manager and above. Only two of our thirteen companies might be said to depart appreciably from this pattern by including a large number of outsiders among their recent high-level appointments, and both of these companies are in the process of creating a program to increase internal management resource development.

Finally, it should also be noted that little difference was found in the perspectives of promotees and decision-makers. They reflected each others' views rather consistently, and the more objective information obtained from both sources was in essential agreement. For this reason, the interpretations that follow embrace the joint contribution of promotees and decision-makers except as specifically noted in context.

Interpretive Highlights

On the basis of what we learned from the perspective of the executives at the top of the organizational pyramid, the following observations were most prominent:

1. Development and succession of the few top managers is more than an extension of the same process that operates in the more numerous intermediate ranks. Hence, top management development requires separate study in its own right.

2. At the top, the group of individuals is relatively small and its members have highly personal relationships. With regard to selection and placement, they interact much as they would in a small company, and a high proportion of group involvement is usual. Informal procedures supplant formal ones. Common consensus is high.

3. The succession to an executive position involves a chain of decisions over a span of years involving individual, group, and organizational variables in interaction. Key decisions that predetermine who will be chosen for an executive position often considerably antedate the final administrative action. Meaningful research of the executive development process needs to incorporate this time dimension and these variables.

4. Most top managers believe that a shortage of executive talent exists and that consequently there is plenty of room at the top for a good man.

5. The distinctions between job description and man description break down at the upper management levels. The man-in-job emerges as a single concept. Moreover, most executives accept the proposition that there is more than one right way of performing a management job.

6. An adequate philosophy of management development cannot concentrate exclusively on manipulation of the individual by selection, appraisal, and training. Several companies made organizational changes to mold a position to the man assigned. This was not considered merely an improvisation to meet contingencies, but a desirable practice. Management organizations *are* structured around people.

7. In order for a man to come up through the ranks to become a top executive of a large corporation, he must move up fast in a relatively short period of time. This is essential if he is to "arrive" equipped with a sufficient range of experience at an age when he will have sufficient time and vitality to do the job. This places a premium upon early discovery and a minimum of delay en route. It also accounts for many of the stresses experienced by the individual and the organization in the management development process.

8. From the corporate view, the value of testing the promising executive candidate early is two-fold: it maximizes his opportunity to learn, and it gives top management the chance

to learn about the individual. Mistakes at junior levels are less costly and easier to rectify than at senior levels.

9. It is essential to the discovery and development of a potential executive that he become visible to top management. Decision-makers depend heavily upon their own assessments of individuals.

10. The diverse needs of a large corporate body and the variety of executives identified with different vested interests usually provide checks and balances, which put a damper on personal favoritism. By and large, demonstrated competence is the most important factor in succession decisions.

11. Special education for upper management most often involves the concept of "broadening." It is not expected to change personality. It is generally directed at building strength on strength and not repairing weaknesses.

12. Formal education or training courses are rarely mentioned as having specific impact upon the way in which an executive performs his job and are never considered as prerequisites for promotion.

The Goal

Although training and development of management-level employees involves one of the major investments of financial resources that organizations make, and managers consistently stress their interest in research on training and development, very few companies are actually conducting such programs. Hence, there is practically no solid information available with which to evaluate present methods of development. This report concludes with a framework for a research program to remedy some of the existing deficiencies.

2

Factors Affecting Top Management Development and Selection

An Overview of the Decision Field

The previous chapter provides part of the general perspective from which we looked at the scene in which management development and succession takes place, and it affords a preview of our findings. We shall now examine the scene in more detail and trace the paths our explorations took as we sought to derive its prominent features from the interviews.

As have many before us, we set out to discover how the decision-makers fit the people-pegs to the position-holes and how in this process they use the facts available to them.

Very quickly we learned that the peg-and-hole-fitting model, even when elegantly embossed with comprehensive position descriptions and electronically generated personnel profiles, does not hold up as a useful way of describing what happens when high-level executives and managers are chosen. It is rare that the textbook prescriptions, adhered to more frequently at lower levels, are followed near the top of the management pyramid. Thus, for example, we do not recall a single instance at the general manager level or above where any of our informants referred to a position description as an important link in the decision process, or where the qualifications

12

of several candidates for a position were laid down side by side and considered step by step.

It soon became apparent that the development and succession of the few top managers is not simply an extension of the same process that governs the selection and progress of the intermediate ranks of management, through which the top managers themselves have passed. Even though there are some common components, the factors affecting the choosing of senior people and the way the decision-making process operates at the top level are different in important respects from the process at the middle range.

In a sense, the situation with respect to selection and placement of top-level executives reverts to the small business context. That is, at the top, the group of individuals is once again relatively small and has highly personal relations, and its members interact as they would in a small company. The individuals generally know each other rather well, or at least some members of the decision-making group can speak about a candidate from close personal contact or direct observation. Hence dependence upon files, figures, and formalities becomes less important. Communication about the people and situations being considered is more direct and more continuous on a day-to-day basis than it is at the lower levels. It also takes place within a more fully shared frame of reference that is capable of taking into meaningful account a larger number of the individualized or unique characteristics of man, motivation, and situation.

In a large organization there is danger that employees will see decisions as being governed by arbitrary conditions imposed by some impersonal source that is psychologically and geographically remote. However, one gets the impression that tolerance of individuality increases at the higher echelons, where the interplay among the parties concerned is more intimate. One also gains the impression that executive appraisal of individuals becomes more realistic and more serious when a direct need exists to fill identifiable, immediate, or prospective vacancies. Then, imperatives of top management responsibility establish the need to examine continually the persons who are prospects in terms of their readiness and fitness to succeed to various alternative senior positions as well as their needs to improve their fitness through assignment and training experiences. This evaluation includes not only the next promotion, but positions several steps further ahead. It is under these circumstances that you are likely to encounter the chief executive officer who, figuratively, and in some cases literally, carries with him an index file of the 50 to 250 top prospects throughout the company, so that he can be prompted to observe and note their performance in action.

This may be contrasted with the picture at middle and lower management levels in a large organization where the number of people and positions becomes awesome and hard for one person to digest, and where simplifying assumptions consequently have to be imposed to make the administrative processes workable. It is probably these simplifying assumptions that make it difficult for "the system" to accommodate the unusual person and the unique situation, and that explain the conformity-inducing pressures that have been the object of popular criticism.

At the middle echelons, too, appraisal that is operationally defined by reference to specific openings is less in evidence. A more general pattern of development is likely to be found because the goals of manager development cannot be as clearly and imperatively defined as can those of top management. This contrast should not be pushed too far. As noted later, promotees were frequently recognized as having executive potential quite early in their careers. In some development programs observed, the pains taken to uncover and advance talented and sometimes atypical people were impressive. However, those cases tend to bring into sharp relief the operational problems involved and emphasize the time and effort required to cope with them.

In our sample of thirteen companies at least, the succession to an executive position rarely involved, at a given point in time, a single decision restricted to who was the best man to fit into a given slot. Instead, it was more likely to be a multifaceted decision affecting managerial resource allocation and reorganization. Although administratively the process tends to be described in terms of the simple geometry of fitting variously shaped pieces together (all represented on the organization chart by rectangles of the same size at a given level), it actually appears to be acted out over some considerable period of time in several, often overlapping, areas which have fluid boundaries.

Certainly the decision-makers are not prone to apply elegant jargon to their actions, but they do give practical recognition to the fact that each change of man-in-job at a top level is a reorganization. Therefore, the way in which a company runs its business may very well be significantly influenced by a change at the top level. Thus a whole barrage of questions is confronted by the decision-makers. These questions may include, but are not limited to, the following:

1. Among the positions that will be open, what appears to be the best allocation of the high-potential people available to us?

2. What are the requirements for each position as now constituted and functioning with the present or recent incumbent?

3. Are the requirements for the future the same? What changes in operations or structure can we anticipate?

4. Do we want to change the way the job is done to meet business objectives? Do we need to accept changes in the way the job is to be done to accommodate the candidate available for the position?

5. How will association with a given group of people in a different situation change the "new" man's behavior?

6. What needs of the organization, including its development of given individuals, must be projected one, three, ten years ahead?

7. What effect will a decision with respect to appointment of Mr. A have upon the opportunities, motivation, and development of others at levels below, above, or coequal with him?

8. How might a decision with respect to the one or several candidates be read by various segments of the corporate "constituency": customers, investors, financiers, creditors, employees, unions, and so on?

Supply and Demand

There is plenty of room at the top. Whether or not this statement can be empirically verified, the top executives we spoke to acted as if it were true. In the eyes of the businessman it almost has to be true, since business and people could always be better.

When positions near the top become vacant, the organization's problem is not so much one of competition among candidates as one of making the best allocation of talent resources. While several people may be considered to fill a given vacancy, they may also be considered for other present and future vacancies. It is not just a question of eliminating one man and accepting another, except, perhaps, when recruiting from outside the company. Most large enterprises are guided by the principle that there is a place for every good man. Find the place or make it, but do not let him get away. The loser in a competition for one position is often the winner in another.

Currently aggravating the supply problem is the well-known population deficit of "depression-babies"—the men now in their thirties who represent the prime executive timber. To make up for the deficit of executives in their fifties and sixties who are dropping out, an accelerated development of younger men is required. Compounding the problem still further is the interruption or deferral of work life as a result of increased military service demands since World War II and the growing numbers of college students going on to graduate work.

The prospect is made no more sanguine by the image of big business in the 1960's in the minds of some of the best college graduates, who regard the challenges and opportunities of a business career as insufficient to excite their interest.[1] Finally, some speculations published in the past few years hold that one impact of computer applications to management will be to reduce seriously the proportion of middle management jobs, and to constrict opportunities for getting experience with the kinds of problems and decisions that will continue to be required at the top of the business.

In the logistics of management development, especially if changes in the characteristics of the input are desired, it is obviously important to initiate action long before the time of anticipated need.

Timing and Sequence

The nature of the factors affecting selection that already have been mentioned indicates the continuing, interlocking, overlapping sequences of decision-making that are continually taking place with respect to executive succession in a large corporation. In our interviews it was difficult to identify a particular time when a key decision was made that determined that Mr. X would be appointed to position Y, whereas a casual observer of only the last step in the decision-making process might easily be misled into believing that most of the choices we studied were made rather perfunctorily. He might think that no more than one candidate was seriously considered, with few of the relevant facts taken into account. He might also be misled by most of the writings on management development. These deal lightly, if at all, with the cumulative incremental series of decisions that ultimately lead to an administrative action that is entered upon the books as *the* decision.

One of our observations that needs stressing is that, with the possible exception of outside recruitment, the actual determining decisions, with regard to most appointments at the executive level, considerably predated official implementation, in some cases by

[1] Thomas J. Watson, Jr., "Business Bridges to the Campus," an address at the Man in Management Award Dinner, Advisory Council of Pace College, Waldorf-Astoria Hotel, New York, N.Y., January 17, 1967.

several years. To be sure, these were not immutable decisions. These initial decisions might be thought of as setting the stage for testing and refining the tentative decision in order to check and confirm it, while allowing room for disconfirmation in a few cases. In the interim the prospective promotee would probably be exposed to more opportunities to prove himself in new assignments to additional decision-makers. During this period, the decision-makers might also engage in informal comparison by looking at some other "potential" and asking: "How does he stack up against our Man A?" The purpose of such an exercise is most often to check and give confidence to the decision-makers rather than to make a thorough comparison with an alternative. In most instances it appeared that by the time of the final choice there was a Man A who was clearly in the lead.

A simplified example of the sequence of events in decision-making might start with the assignment of a person to the job of assistant to a corporate officer, with the intention, if he acquitted himself well, of making him executive vice-president of a subsidiary. An individual is not usually appointed to this position unless he is acknowledged to be the heir apparent of the incumbent president. And so the presidential succession in this case began to take rather firm shape with the selection for the "assistant to" position.

Of course, allowance is made for unforeseen contingencies. New people, circumstances, and information may emerge in the interval between the tentative and the final decision. A new subsidiary may be established for which Man A is the best-equipped presidential material, or the sudden departure of an incumbent officer or a prime candidate for another job may demand recasting.

There is nothing rigid about the sequences with regard to timing of moves, path of movement between assignments, or key jobs in a career. These were found to vary from company to company and from time to time.

This all adds up to the following impressions:

1. The process of forging a decision about the choice of a senior officer of a large organization or organizational unit often reaches back a long way.

2. The most vital links in the chain may be found at different points in the time-span for different people.

3. Analysis of executive development and succession within the narrow time-span surrounding a recent selection, such as the particular events that took place at the conference table, will not be useful.

4. In an attempt to provide a simple model, current concepts suffer from compression of the time perspective. There is a crucial need for research on executive career development that covers longer time-spans than have been studied in the past.

Appraisal

Every management development program has a way of keeping score, though not always in a formal way. Again, variation is great. At one end of the spectrum is the situation where the head of each organizational unit initiates his own search for managers and makes each choice, subject only to veto by management at a higher level. At the other end of the spectrum is the situation in which a panel functions at a high level, meeting regularly to engage in a three-dimensional chess game, moving men around to anticipate and meet the needs of the total corporate management structure. At the levels we are discussing, the situation will usually lie somewhere between these two poles.

A high proportion of group involvement is usual, though not in every case formalized by standing committees or ad hoc panels. Although in most situations the immediate supervisor has a strong voice and a defined or tacit veto power in selection of his subordinates, it is apparent that less than complete decision-making autonomy is exercised by individuals where the corporate management involvement cuts across organizational boundaries. Several cases in point were called to our attention. These include one case where there was an attempt to take into account in the decision-making not only the immediate assignment under consideration, but also the candidate's prospective assignment after that. In another case, career plans for individuals were laid out in four-year units that might embrace one to three prospective changes in assignment.

The performance rating illustrates a chronic problem. When the purpose of appraisal is to fill a specific position at a given level, the appraisers generally have a pretty good idea about what kind of person would fit the bill. They are realistic. They know that probably no one will fit it perfectly. They make comparisons among those available candidates who best approximate the requirements. A phrase coined by an interviewee applies here: "competitive competency"; being better than the others available at a given level, at a given time and place, in the areas most relevant to the vacant position. With the available position to examine, it is relatively easy to narrow the field of principal contenders. This is the situation that is more often found at the higher management levels.

In the most classic application of this approach that was observed, no general performance ratings were used. Instead, an intense review of management staffing requirements and career planning was conducted at all levels to identify prospects for each position in management. The outcome was revised and reviewed with top management at least once each year.

Contrast this with the familiar circumstances attending most formalized performance ratings, more likely to be utilized at middle and lower management ranks. In the absence of the frame of reference set by a specific assignment, the rater is called upon to apply rather abstract definitions of characteristics to one ratee at a time, with only idealized norms provided. This generates attitudes of rater and ratee that become personalistic rather than objective-centered. When the time comes for decision, it is difficult to interpret the data in the context of a given opening. As a consequence, both parties become unhappy about the whole process, and sometimes they displace this dissatisfaction upon one another. One attempt to provide a specific frame of reference at the junior management level involved evaluations made at the first level of management in terms of abilities necessary to succeed five years later at the third level of management in a district manager job. Also, from almost the beginning of their careers in the company, ratings of individuals are made in the form of predictions of the ultimate level to which they will rise, up to vice-president. Then work situations are used along the way to test these predictions.

One thing that tends to salvage performance appraisal systems is that the most and the least outstanding individuals are easily identifiable. Hence, even relatively crude systems will correctly identify a high proportion of good executive candidates, since the selection ratio is inherently stringent. Of course, for the corporate interest, early discovery of outstanding management prospects is the main objective.

In the relatively small circle of top management, group participation is useful in improving the reliability of communication with regard to the performance of the individual. Simultaneously, it improves mutual understanding of the critical performance requirements of positions being considered. Because decision-makers with different needs and viewpoints are involved, checks are built in that offer some protection against slanting appraisals in any single direction.

These considerations can rarely proceed very far without involving organization aims and structure. In a large organization, the frequency of managerial replacement helps to insure constant and current consideration of these matters and helps to maintain a moving consensus as a dynamic frame of reference for organization development and management development decisions. It helps the participants keep in touch with each other, with the kind of jobs key people are doing, and with the problems and needs of the corporation. As a result, the final appraisal and choice comes about over a period of time through an evolutionary decision process that brings to the fore one or two contenders for a given position. At this point the decision-makers express little need for reference to standard data files or a formalized procedure.

As for the subjects of these appraisals, most of them seemed to feel that they knew how they stood with their bosses, and discussions with their superiors confirmed that they were reasonably accurate. However, the feedback seldom could be credited to use of existing performance appraisal procedures, and never at high management levels. A large degree of ambiguity entered the picture when a bright management prospect was told what his future potential was considered to be. It seemed acceptable to display the panorama of opportunity, but not to say much about where the individual might be placed in it. The decision-makers seemed to imply that unwanted behavioral changes would accompany such disclosures. One wonders if it is motivationally sound to expect an individual to involve himself deeply in all aspects of his organization's development without knowing his own part in its future. There appears to be need for an objective answer to the question of what are the good and bad effects of the company's disclosure of its expectations for individual executives.

The Man-in-Job Unit

As the scope of a general manager's responsibility increases, the descriptions of the job and of the man holding the job become merged into one description of man-in-job. This is recognized by top management and gives great saliency to the need for constantly appraising the man as part of the process of determining the way in which the job can best be performed and how man and job should be developed together.

The relatively infrequent reference to coaching or similarly specific preparation by superiors immediately before or after a promotion is made may be partly explained by the feeling at top management level that each executive, after being judged ready to assume a certain level of responsibility, should be free to develop his own style. This almost seems an acceptance of the proposition that there is no one right way of managing. Examples were cited of two people who had run the same job in very different but equally effective ways. For the person who has moved up from an immediately subordinate position, it might be taken for granted that he has already learned what he needs to know to move up a step. But we have not noticed that specific preparation is given any more frequently to people who come from a different sector of the organization, or even from outside. "Here is the problem; you fix it," is the way one person typified the frequent approach to a promotee. Some promotees volunteered that they were just as glad to have it so.

What at first may seem an anomalous view was summed up by an interviewee, who maintained that a mixture of good intelligence and specific ignorance is desirable in moving into a new position: it creates a climate where asking questions is acceptable, ready answers are not expected, and obvious dependence upon others helps to establish rapport with new associates. Others made the point that managers at higher levels need not necessarily have complete knowledge of day-to-day operations of the unit they manage if adequate operating skills exist within it. They included some examples of how they secured a strong position with new subordinates, including those who had been passed over, by quickly crediting them with special competence and reinforcing this by appropriate delegation. Some also suggested that because they lacked thorough technical knowledge in a given area they had to learn to put things in plain language, and that their ability to do this made them better communicators in translating technical content into top management language.

The man-in-top-job functions largely autonomously. He exercises considerable discretionary authority without direct instruction or control. His competence is judged for the most part by his effectiveness in working with people at all levels, but clear-cut measures are not available on this kind of effectiveness. Hence, the top manager has to have complete confidence that the promotee is an extension of his own competence. The unavailability of detailed checks or controls creates a heightened sensitivity to the interpersonal, intraorganizational compatability of the individual. It induces a subjective psychological demand upon the decision-maker for a very personal involvement, for which there can be no objective empirical substitute. This is so because the decision-maker is at once judge, jury, and attorney. His is the definition, the test, and the criterion of ultimate validity. Therefore, those who make critical decisions on management succession appear to regard as crucial the requirement that they have confidence in their personal knowledge of the competence of the man they have chosen, or at least in the person who endorses that individual.

Rate of Advance

When we look back over the road traveled by the promotees to whom we spoke, one of the things that stands out is how fast the candidate for the top corporate positions must move if he is to come up through the ranks of a large corporation and "arrive," equipped with a sufficient range of experience, and at an age when he will have sufficient time and vitality left to do the job. The bigger and more diversified the company, the faster he must move.

The all-embracing problem facing the candidate for a top corporate position is that only those who get on the track early, and stay close to the main line almost continuously, stand a chance of making it to the top in time. For the aspirant this means that he can ill afford delays en route. On the one hand, this may be interpreted to mean that sidetracks are to be avoided, and that adventures in innovation and nonconformity involve risk of derailment. On the other hand, this may be read to mean that one should be alert for shortcuts that will reduce the number and duration of stops along the way, that these great leaps forward often constitute high-risk, high-gain situations. Indeed, there are examples of success achieved by both routes. When one compares case histories of those who have achieved high positions by following these two routes, they seem to have in common an unbroken string of successes on the way up. Allowing that we only dealt directly with the successful people, and that rationalization or selective recall may screen out whatever is contradictory to the success image, one wonders whether a more complete study would actually show that one setback is enough to remove an individual from contention in "sudden death" competition.

On management's side there are also problems, of course. Some decision-maker interviewees made observations about the demand for many adaptations. For example, a record of winning all the contests might not be altogether good. It left the company without an estimate of how a person might react if he lost. Some of the successful people, they said, could become too sure of themselves. Some might lack humility and exhibit frustration as they moved up from direct-action situations into positions where action needed to be implemented through several layers of management. In the words of an interviewee: "It's hard to adjust after being on the firing line." Some, it was felt, had to learn how to lose, or might profit in maturity by facing a situation in which they "had their teeth kicked in." There are nasty situations, it was pointed out, where you literally cannot win, yet somebody must handle them. There is need to guard against conditioning people to work for the applause rather than the accomplishment. As articulated by one senior executive: "Until a fellow experiences how it feels to be a 'loser' he is not fully qualified to control the lives of others."

For management the evidence provided by the successes and rapid advancement of many comparatively young people raises some pointed questions. Most would agree that premium abilities and intense application can shorten the time necessary for learning the essentials of a job, but *how* and *how much* is not clear. Knowledge of the business and of general management practices is a basic requirement. But for the subjects of this study, such knowledge had for the most part become a common denominator that no longer provided much grounds for differentiation. More information is needed concerning how much of what types of experience provide a satisfactory base for movement into upper management ranks. Much has been said about how the man makes the job; not as much has been said about how the job can make the man. Men of this quality provide many examples of their capacity to assimilate experience and to learn quickly a new area of work. The surprise that often greets the achievement of a person thrown into a job that was thought to be too big for him raises questions about what gap there ought to be between a man's present status and his next assignment in order to optimize his development and the company's gain. There may be too few "giant steps" or too many "baby steps" built into executive development programs. There certainly seems to be potential profit in the further careful study of characteristics, motivations, and adaptations of those who seek and succeed in this rapidly paced race to the corporate summit.

Individual and Organizational Stress

Among some of the managers in our sample we find a sensitivity to the stress imposed on both individuals and organizations when many steps in the career ladder have to be climbed in a relatively short work life. There is concern that the best utilization may not be made of potentially high-level management talents as a result of too few people being brought into the talent pool, or owing to their being kept out or eliminated for nonvalid reasons. All of these limitations may have unhappy consequences for individuals, and, of equal consequence, they may artificially restrict the company's range of choice. The concern expressed consistently related to the previously mentioned problem that too often time does not permit those who got a late start, or got off the track for a while, to catch up. The next express is already passing with a new load of hopefuls. Few top management development systems schedule a follow-up to pick up stragglers and late arrivals, or to see if an individual who made a mistake or was overlooked in his earlier years has now become a worthy competitor. Except when severe shortages exist, attention tends to be given exclusively to those who are out front in the race.

We should note that what has just been said is offered in the framework of a career within a single corporate structure and a policy of promotion from within. It may be that one of the shortcut routes to the top, or a way to make up for lost time, is to move to another company. There, given entry with some reputation for success achievements and the inclination of the new set of decision-makers to think well of their own choices, obstacles to progress may thus be circumvented or earlier sins and errors more readily obscured. Therefore, one starts with a clean slate viewed through rose-colored glasses.

The number of outside recruits that we met was too small to develop further discussion of this group.

Situational-Organizational Variables

An adequate philosophy of management development cannot concentrate exclusively on manipulation of the individual by selection, appraisal, and training. To be oblivious to the requirement for concomitant consideration and manipulation of the situational-organizational variables that may help or hinder development is to incur the risk of built-in organizational mediocrity.

Although one will not find in any company's management development handbook anything about changing organization to mold positions to conform to the man assigned, this was done in several places that were visited. In some cases, this was not considered merely an improvisation to meet contingencies, but a desirable practice. Management organizations *are* structured around people. It *is* easier to change charts than it is to change people.

Thus, we have the example of a company whose top management definitions of assignment were kept fluid enough to create places for as many highly promising people as possible during a period of rapid growth. In another setting, a common practice was for a person, after being promoted, to maintain some of his former responsibilities until his successor was ready to assume them. When a ready replacement is not available, management may change structure to eliminate a position. Some men are put in a new senior position in order to set it up, with the understanding that it can be turned over to someone else. Where the prevailing management philosophy is that decisions should be made at the lowest possible level of organization in order to maximize early development, the total structure must be built accordingly. We have also seen that businesses are bought and mergers accomplished with the avowed aim of acquiring new management talent. Nor is it unknown for reorganizations to be effected to take advantage of some individual's peculiar pattern of abilities or to get around roadblocks in high places. In some places advisory positions have been created to keep the experience of veteran executives available as well as to recognize their long-standing contributions, while not impeding the advance of younger elements.

A final illustration involves the case of several promotees who expressed surprise that they had been chosen for their positions. Their astonishment was quite legitimate; a top executive testified that in the "dog-eat-dog" atmosphere that had prevailed only a few years ago, these democratically minded, people-centered gentlemen would probably not have been considered sufficiently combative to survive.

Most people know better than to take an organization chart at face value. They recognize that in order to fully comprehend how a given organization really works the network of informal influence must be known.

For each corporation the need to move people up (in level) and around (in breadth and variety of experience) raises a host of decisions, some of which are treated as broad policy decisions and some of which are dealt with on a case-by-case basis.

Corporate Versus Divisional Benefits

As characterized by a recently promoted vice-president, "the executive development program is a system to identify people for *corporate* consumption." There often exists in large organizations a built-in conflict involving problems of trade-off between benefits to the organization as a whole, benefits to component units of the organization, and benefits to individuals. The question of how to create and maintain a prevailing corporation-centered orientation embraces issues of rare delicacy.

We encountered a great deal of discussion by top management concerning the relative merits of having promising managers move up within a single operational segment or field of specialization, with selection and training for general management taking place later in their careers, as opposed to starting them early on a range of assignments that provide equipment for later general management duties, even though the individual may not get as fully immersed in any particular aspect of operations or management. Similarly, the executives wrestled with the question of whether it is better to have an individual spend more time in a relatively small number of jobs or shorter periods of time in a greater number of jobs. In companies where the latter condition obtained the question was raised as to whether it is possible to get a fair appraisal of the quality of a man's performance if he is in a position for only a few years. He may move out of his job before his mistakes have time to catch up with him. On the other side of the coin is the question of whether there is time to make an adequate estimate of his positive assets and achievements for future reference.

A strong argument that was advanced in favor of relatively early assignment to positions of responsibility is that from the company's standpoint at least, the risks are less if mistakes are made early when corrective action is easier to accomplish. If a misassignment is made at a more senior level, the costs of error are greater, as are the organizational and personal readjustment difficulties involved.

In the same vein, disfavor was expressed regarding positions established, or assignments rotated, to serve principally a training function. To satisfy the individual's motivation as well as the company's need for substantial performance information, a shift was indicated away from "watching" toward "doing" and learning by doing "real" work.

Corporations in which career development programs are run independently by major fields of specialization, divisions, or subsidiaries, without much integration across internal organization lines, tend to experience more difficulty in meeting needs for corporate officers with adequately broad general management experience and outlook. Complaints are frequently voiced by corporate executives that people who move up through single subsidiaries, divisions, or specialties to the level of vice-president or general manager tend to be more limited in background, more parochial in outlook, and more advanced in age than is desirable in a corporate officer. This confronts the decision-makers with a deficit in relevant performance information on which to base an estimate of further potential for success and imposes upon the individual an excessive requirement late in the game for on-the-job learning under pressure.

Some top executives voiced the criticism of these contentions that those who see themselves primarily in the role of professional managers, with general managerial skills that are transferable to a multitude of operational situations, are less disposed to identify with or develop loyalty to individual organizations or organizational units. "Professional helmsman," was the label applied by one board chairman. They are seen to measure their achievements against outside professional criteria rather than against the inside organizational values. To some this means that they are self-centered rather than organization-centered.

In almost every corporation one can point out executives who are development-oriented and those who are not. Well-planned discovery and development, of course, means having more of the former type in an organization. Some decision-makers mention that one of the things they look for is whether there is a demand for people who work under a particular manager. Some promotees attribute much of their early impetus to the growth conditions provided by a certain supervisor. One vividly described the "Homer

Roger College" (name substituted) and the disproportionate number of the company's present managers who were alumni of the organizational unit of which Homer Roger had been manager for a long time. Others offered similar examples. Where these kinds of achievements are recognized and rewarded, there appear to be fewer complaints about intracompany hoarding or raiding of management talent. Instead a pride in developing people is exhibited and a demand for one's subordinates, though creating some administrative problems, is looked upon as a mark of distinction. In this organizational climate the integrity of the corporate executive development system is less prone to be subverted and discredited by the practice of palming off rejects to other organizational units. However, on the whole, rewards for personnel development are more often discussed as a goal than applied in practice.

Large Versus Small Division Benefits

One will usually find a difference in outlook toward the foregoing issues between large and small organizational divisions.

The large divisions are more self-sufficient in their talent inventory than the latter. Hence they are less enamored of cooperative, transdivisional, corporate personnel development plans. They are more often alarmed that other divisions are raiding their best people and giving little in return.

The smaller units, of which the corporate staff is usually one and with which it is usually allied on this issue, are less self-sufficient. In their smaller talent pools, they more often find a lack of the particular type of person they need. Also, they cannot offer as wide a range and number of opportunities to their people. Therefore, they must look to other divisions both as sources of management talent and as growth opportunity outlets for their people. They will be found lined up on the side of cooperative development programs most of the time.

Accomplishment Versus Development Objectives

Tied in with many of the questions that have gone before is one that asks whether the purposes of the organization are better served by making either the more immediate operational accomplishments or the longer-term development objectives the greater determinant in assignment of managers. Related to this is the determination of whether, in development and succession, the paramount consideration shall be either that of sustaining a planned developmental assignment scheme or of filling position needs as they arise, with operational requirements having priority claim. In neither of these conditions are the policies and procedures absolute. Trade-offs, in terms of expected long- and short-term benefits, are constantly made. But the policy stance assumed by top management certainly does materially influence the probability with which alternative patterns of decisions will emerge over time, and thus it shapes operations as well as management development programs and procedures.

The question of how old the top management echelon should be is related to the preceding points. Obviously, it makes a difference whether the company's answer is 45–50 or 60–65.

The Crown Prince

The issue of the "crown prince" is largely academic since the proposition almost universally accepted by those at present in top positions, as expressed by one of them, is that "the system must pick out the 'crown princes,' whether you like the term or not." It is necessary and desirable to identify the top management candidates early in their careers so that proper testing, observation, and grooming can be planned in the limited time available. Because many come and few are chosen, this inevitably raises the prospect that a dichotomy of "Ins" and "Outs" will be created. The happy Ins are few and the less happy Outs are many. It is difficult to establish a balance that provides that those who may have been overlooked originally will have another opportunity to be considered, if their performance merits it, and yet does not hold out frustrating, empty promises to many more than can be chosen.

In order to realize the long-term potential benefits to the organization, the intervening obstacles to organizational harmony must be negotiated. It is all very well to say that not every employee wants to or expects to be president. Indeed, only a few of our promotees gave signs of having deliberately calculated to reach career targets at their current position or beyond. Most insisted that they had concentrated on doing each job well, expecting future advancement to take care of itself or be taken care of by the powers that be. Nonetheless, few creatures of our striving society acknowledge a willingness to stand pat with what they have won in the achievement derby. People become peevish when it is made obvious that some people are being given special treatment while others are being taken for granted.

How big and how real is the problem posed by these stresses? It is difficult to estimate this from discussions limited to those who succeed. The planners and decision-makers do talk about these issues rather freely. It would be helpful to have more normative data on relevant attitudes.

In attempting to blunt the sharp edges of conflict that are inherent in this dilemma, management resorts to a variety of subterfuges. The most well known is the substitution of title for influence. These subterfuges probably serve some legitimate purposes, except where management inclines toward self-delusion and hides from the real issues instead of objectively coping with them. It is hard to visualize any circumstance where early identification of management talent would not raise the spectre of the crown prince and elitism. Nor is this limited to the early years of employment. It involves any situation where a substantial, planned, lead time in development for management posts exists.

3

Factors Affecting the "Take-Off" to Top Management

If there is any one factor that can be said to account for the difference in the way the typical management development system functions at the upper echelons and the way it functions at the lower echelons, it is the corporate officer's belief that the system's chief purpose is to bring to light those who have the makings of a corporate executive; and the sooner the better.

Visibility

Once the "comer" is spotted by top management, he moves into a different orbit in which the standard operating procedures of the development system are superseded by another set of procedures. These are usually more encompassing in scope but less structured in practice and involve the direct intervention and involvement of senior management to a considerably greater degree. That is, the point at which an individual becomes visible to top management in a favorable light is the "take-off" point in the career path to top management, and it is the point where top management pretty much takes over in order to test and groom the candidates. In this sense, one can say that there are two systems in effect: a general management development program, and a specific executive development system.

The failure to recognize the distinction between the two systems may explain some of the apparent inconsistencies in the views expressed by decision-makers. Their critical statements tended to be attached to the routines of the management *development* system (for example, ratings, inventories, reports, interviews, standard tests, and so on). However, management *review,* in which the senior executives themselves participated as decision-makers, was viewed differently and was not often thought of as part of the management development system, even where the same staff originated the procedures and guided their implementation.

This may account for the following statements made by decision-makers in corporations that had extensive and influential management development programs: "Management development is an operational responsibility that is too important to be delegated to staff." "When the system becomes stylized, there is a strong tendency to concentrate not upon doing the job, but to engage in the game of beating the system."

In some of the more sophisticated management development programs, cognizance is taken of the different needs and purposes that prevail at two or more levels, and for the topmost level, a high potential group is defined and a plan designed that is especially suited to the small numbers of managers and positions on this select list.

It is clear that the recommendations and decisions of senior executives largely direct and control the actual course of management development and succession, as sometimes distinguished from the theoretically prescribed course toward the top. It seems equally clear that the effective exercise of the senior executives' roles in management development demands that they be able to *see* and identify meaningful and appropriate differences in employees. The conditions that determine visibility and the influence of visibility factors upon development and advancement of top managers figures so prominently in the picture painted for us by interviewees that the visibility dimension merits a full discussion in this report.

The Search for Distinguishing Characteristics

Decision-makers experience difficulty in finding objective differences in highly select groups. As a consequence, trivial and superficial differences among candidates often determine the choice. In the absence of more solid evidence, these differences can assume great weight because of the decision-makers' need to establish some distinction and to rationalize their decision. Thus, the choice is not necessarily a reflection of the empirical or logical validity of the items of information.

It has been demonstrated by research under a great variety of conditions and with many kinds of groups, including boards of directors, that the manner in which a leader differentiates the characteristics of his most and least preferred co-workers bears a relationship to the operational effectiveness of his group's performance.[1] On the basis of the interviews, we can assert that the ability to identify and cultivate the characteristics of people who can do a good job for you is attributed to successful executives. However, developing this ability in specific people and applying it in specific situations continues to present difficulties.

A few large corporations have conducted research on early identification of management talent. However, these have concentrated on the early years.

Lacking ideal methods for identification of executive talent, and without much empirical support for the assumption that long-range predictions can be made with practical and useful accuracy, the decision-makers must still depend upon their own assessments, even if their confidence in the validity of their own assessments is shaky.

---

[1] See F. E. Fiedler, "A Contingency Model of Leadership Effectiveness," in L. Berkowitz, ed., *Advances in Social Psychology*, I (New York: Academic Press, 1964), pp. 150–190; and E. P. Godfrey, F. E. Fiedler, and D. M. Holl, *Boards, Managers, and Company Success* (Danville, Ill.: Interstate Press and Publishers, 1959).

The Importance of Being in the Right Place at the Right Time

Because the circumstances attending personnel appraisal and promotion decisions are seen by most of those concerned as being loosely structured and unreliable, luck is frequently credited as a determinant of choice. Recurrent in interviews with decision-makers, and even more so with promotees, is the theme of being in the right place at the right time.

Ideally, in an inventory of managers, one would like to have tests, records, interviews, references, and so forth, that would infallibly identify those who will make it to the top. A major proportion of the top executives with whom we spoke emphasized the desirability of being able to identify future executives early. A few wistfully expressed the hope of finding a test that could help. However, we do not have any substantial data on the accuracy that may be expected from long-range predictions.

To be sure, individual destinies are not completely controlled either by the individual or by the corporation. Wars break out, executives have heart attacks, mergers are frustrated by antitrust action, inflation occurs, technology induces sudden changes, and new competitors appear upon the scene. These events have considerable unplanned influence on the organizational success criteria, and may even have a bearing upon evaluations of individuals who, rightly or wrongly, are identified with an organization's up or down movements. Of interest here is the number of promotees who came to prominence because of a part they played in a significant corporate reorganization episode.

The best-laid plans often need to be rethought and rejuggled. Provision for timely reviews and revision is an inherent part of good planning. Natural uncertainties cannot obscure the fact that being in the right place at the right time may be translated as very largely a matter of being in some way injected into a situation that provides opportunity to be visible to a person who is currently, or who will subsequently become, a key decision-maker.

Accidental Versus Planned Discovery

Planning that provides for adequate opportunity for potential promotees to be seen by the right people under a variety of conditions quite naturally aids the development and succession processes. At a premium in most companies are positions that provide a good opportunity for a manager, particularly a young manager, to have sufficient weight and range of independent responsibility to provide a significant test of his executive ability. Certain jobs can be identified as gate-opening positions. People who are assigned to those positions relatively early in their careers, and who are often already viewed as the "comers," get good visibility. If they do well in these positions, they are marked for and move toward better things. Management recognition of the need for such positions is mentioned rather often, particularly in companies where operations are highly integrated (such as oil companies) in contrast to those where multiple profit centers exist (as illustrated by retail chains with many stores and departments).

A deficiency of gate-opening positions in a firm may seriously impede the management appraisal and development system. Lack of opportunity to observe "real" performance increases dependence upon transitory, adventitious, superficial, fractionated, and personalistic grounds for choice by executives, and it decreases the reliability and validity of the decision-making process.

Where lack of a sufficient number of these important positions exists, sometimes positions have been improvised, or task forces have been put to work on a problem, in order to provide a test and evaluation opportunity for given individuals. Sometimes these needs have even influenced more extensive corporate reorganization in the form of new organizational units, increased decentralization, profit-center organization, and a flattened organizational pyramid.

Management is generally aware that the provision for visibility is important in the management development and succession process. In one way or another the top management decision-makers in our sample consistently stressed the importance of potential top managers being in positions where their abilities would be manifested and their performances could be assessed by key decision-makers. They were concerned that people of prospective merit for management were being overlooked in nonvisible assignments. In general, this concern applied to the lower ranks. Several times executives emphasized their deliberate efforts to create opportunities to see promising people in action. To illustrate, in some instances they have put out advance word to field units they were going to visit that more people at a junior level should be given leading roles at conferences and presentations. At other times they have arranged to travel with "comers." In the upper ranks, more frequent personal interaction in the normal course of business minimizes the possibility of oversight. Yet there are even examples of problems in this context, such as the one posed by executives assigned outside of the United States (increasingly including nationals of other countries).

The difference between the more and less highly developed management development systems is the difference between accidental, fortuitous discovery of management talent and the continuous planned campaign of discovery. The former condition is much more likely to be found where there is a heavy dependence upon outside recruitment to fill senior executive positions. In organizations with comprehensive developmental programs, considerable pains are taken to provide opportunities for visibility and thus guard against oversight.

The rationale for the psychological testing of managers, particularly at junior levels, is frequently not that it is a basis for specific selection "in," "up," or "out," but that it is a check to help insure that good people have not been submerged and ignored and that they have been encouraged and helped to develop themselves.

Similarly, it is a frequent practice to assign likely candidates from operating units or subsidiaries to a position on the corporate staff for a period of time. This provides exposure of the corporation to the man so that he can learn and, more important, exposure of the man to the corporate executives so that they can learn about him.

In the upper echelons, as indicated above, promotion decisions are themselves highly visible. The people chosen and their actions and performances are more open to public view than those at lower levels. Their successes and failures represent large profits and costs. Good or poor choices may then reflect credit or discredit upon the decision-makers. Hence, it defies credibility to expect that top executives will surrender even a modicum of direct and personal involvement in these decisions or give much weight to any facts that they do not completely understand and cannot confidently and comfortably assimilate in their thinking processes.

Principles of Visibility

So far, our discussion, including the section on the conditions likely to affect a person's visibility, has been generally from the top down. But the interviews also provided much material bearing on what the individual may do on his own account to improve his visibility. Drawing from the views of those at the top as they look back on their rise from the bottom up to their present position, here are some generalizations that we have made which we will call "principles of visibility."

The "hitch your wagon to a star" principle is demonstrated rather frequently. It holds that if a previous superior, whom you have favorably impressed, moves up in the organization, your chances of following him up the ladder at some time in the future are increased. A tally of the number of times a promotee in the sample had earlier been a subordinate of one or more of those involved in choosing him for promotion—in some instances several times—would add up to an impressive percentage of cases. There are, of course, exceptions to this principle. Too close an identification with a falling star can be hazardous, and there are instances where a superior's possessiveness boxed in a protégé.

The "big fish in the little pond" principle holds that, given two individuals equal in quality of past performance and potential and at the same hierarchical level, he who works in a smaller unit of organization, a less populous community, or a more geographically separate location, is more likely to be visible to key decision-makers. Perhaps an additional factor helps this individual to profit career-wise by an outstandingly effective performance in this kind of situation. It may be possible that the people in out-of-the-way places only occasionally become visible to the upper management and that their smaller successes and failures may be given less notice, so that a brilliant performance shines more brightly than might otherwise be the case. (Of course, the converse would be true for a costly ineffective performance; but we have not talked much about the nonachievers.)

As indicated, the "little pond" can have many forms and locations. All of them do not have to be directly work related. A man's civic activities may contribute to his image as one who is a leader or who has developed good political connections that can be useful to the company. Similarly, prominence in professional organizations can lend the weight of peer recognition to an individual's worth, and in turn, his status is seen as reflecting credit upon the organization that employs him.

The "hew to the line" principle reflects a consensus that, where comparisons and choices are made, the odds favor the man on the line. Although good performance in a corporate staff position is often a necessary condition for further advancement it may not be a sufficient condition. "A corporate staff job is not a place to get glory," said one interviewee. A good staff man can be most appreciated for his special contributions to the work of others, but the "results" are identified with the operating executives, and so the contribution of the staff executive may lose something in translation. The dogma that pervades management bibles reinforces the line-staff dichotomy and the priority accorded the former.

A great deal of the staff executive's activities involve relationships across-the-board organizationally, but it has been pointed out to us that this may leave him bereft of any key figure in the power network who identifies the staff man as his protégé and provides the strong sponsorship necessary to advance his cause. Therefore, it is no surprise that among rising executives, whose sights are on the management pinnacle, a wary eye is cast upon premature offers of staff assignments or extended tenure in such assignments. A staff position would be premature or too extended where it threatened to create a "good staff man" image before a reputation as a "good operating manager" was firmly established. Movement by the operating or technical person into staff activities at an advanced level is relatively frequent; movement by a person with chiefly staff experience into operational management at an advanced level is, on the average, less frequent. This trend is obvious to everyone and accounts for the wariness.

Of course, there are some good staff men who are afforded opportunities to move into the line at a relatively late stage of their careers. However, comment on these cases most often included an element of *taking a chance* in spite of their deficiency in operating experience. One decision-maker interviewed said that "the danger that a man might be classified as a specialist all of his life" was illustrated by a case in which he spent six months convincing other decision-makers that an excellent staff executive should be given the chance to make the transition to a line position that was vacant. He also noted the surprise that accompanied the man's rapid and successful assumption of the new duties.

The "new look" principle is presumed to be correlated with the foregoing: an individual is likely to draw disproportionate attention, and to loom more prominently in the perception of key decision-makers, if he is assigned to a task, unit, or organization that is distinctly different in some respect from that which is customary or conventional in degree or kind for the firm. Such a situation is likely to represent, literally or perceptually, a "high risk–high gain" condition. Lack of precedents, models, standards, or benchmarks are likely to induce anxieties in top managers. These uncertainties cause them to see in the situation greater than normal complexity, unpredictability, difficulty, and risk, and lead them to be conservative in expectations of the individual's success. So "enhancement by contrast" works in favor of the person who performs well in these circumstances. As one general manager said: "People involved in problem situations get to be better known." Or more succinctly put by another: "Crises create heroes."

One related, more specific illustration of enhancement by contrast was the case of an individual succeeding to a job that was badly performed by his predecessor. One interviewee rather clearly articulated his rationale for accepting such a position while others were avoiding it. He felt that he could not miss because the new man would have little chance of going anywhere but up. The needs and means for change were already quite obvious to him. The support of higher management was fairly well assured, and the relief at getting rid of the "bad apple" would add a pink glow to the estimates of the new man's accomplishments. This individual also pointed out how to augment the new look by bringing in new subordinates. In fact, he traded upon the crisis situation to get backing to compete for higher quality subordinates, thus again taking advantage of the odds in his favor.

Another aspect of enhancement by contrast is illustrated in the situation where an individual moves out of an area of previous specialization into an area that seems to be at least technically different from the first. Because higher-ups regard him as operating with a handicap on the new assignment—limited education, technical knowledge, or specialized experience in operations—if he makes a go of it, his achievement is more likely to be noted and praised than the achievement of the man who starts out with credentials that better match the job. Another example is the individual who has acquired some special competence that is rare in the company (fortuitously or by deliberate foresight), which is unveiled in a timely way with widespread impact. Application of computer technology to management and operations was quite frequently referred to in this connection.

Implicit in this "new look" principle is the assumption that the upcoming manager is not content to play it safe. In getting ahead he must equate calculated risk with challenge and seek it.

The "make up your mind" principle represents a factor that overlaps all others. It says that organizational visibility is associated with making important decisions. Of course, decisions can be good ones or poor ones, and one is judged by his batting average or runs batted in. Good judgment is essential. Poor judgment is sometimes pardonable. But failure to make judgments, or chronic indecision, is a fatal flaw. An individual does not have a chance if he just stands there and does not swing. The fellow who would fill the shoes of an executive has to show that he can make up his mind even in the face of considerable uncertainty.

This analogy must be credited to the promotee who attributed his success to having "hit a long ball early in the game." He was referring here to the impression he made after only a few months in the company because of his ability to assemble facts, assess the situation, pose the appropriate questions, and offer good alternatives, in a fashion that created surprise among the executives because it was not expected of one with so little experience.

The decision-makers are scouting for people who, like themselves, can assume the responsibility for making and living with their decisions, even if they must subsequently alter these decisions as they are tested by additional facts and new circumstances. These decision-makers gave many examples of their esteem for those who measured up in this fashion and their displeasure with those who did not.

The principle of "misplaced modesty" suggests that self-effacement is not altogether appropriate for the aspiring executive. Other things being equal, an individual can significantly influence his own corporate destiny by discreetly developing his visibility. This does not mean that he exaggerates his accomplishments and hides or explains away his mistakes, aspires to infallibility, or derogates his peers. It does mean that he accepts the fact that, in addition to doing a good job, it is important that "somebody up there knows me." This may be accomplished by taking various initiatives: by soliciting counsel from the personnel management development staff or upper management echelons; by indicating availability for positions that might not usually be considered directly relevant to one's background and experience, or what was known of it (particularly if the move would tend to create more of a generalist image); by contributing extra or unique unsolicited efforts, reports, suggestions, and so on; by participating in extracurricular professional or civic activities; by exercising available assignment options that will make one a more prominent figure in a particular setting and/or put one in closer proximity to a key executive.

The principle of "performance paramountcy" holds that, in the final analysis, demonstrated performance carries more weight than connections. This does not contradict what has been already established, namely, that in addition to what you know and how you show you can use it, who knows you is important—or to paraphrase an interviewee, "Nothing succeeds like success—and a strong patron." But the connections can run from decision-makers to prospective promotees, as is recognized by methods introduced in several companies to establish such connections. One president interviewed carries the names of prospective promotees with him on his travels. One company indoctrinated its executives with the philosophy that they were to regard themselves as assistants to their immediate subordinates in fostering growth. In another case, members of the board of directors had specific responsibility for keeping abreast of management needs, prospects, and development planning activities, in a given part of the corporation. These forms of sponsorship exemplify means that are used to systematize and objectify without depersonalizing connections, while seeking to eliminate the stigma of personal politics voiced in the old complaint, "It's not what you know, but who you know that counts." Among some executives there seems to be hypersensitivity on this point. They label as politics all social-psychological dynamics in the organizational culture, without discriminating between constructive and nonconstructive aspects. This may explain why objective analyses of these important factors in executive careers has mostly remained on a sidetrack.

The variety of needs of a large corporate body, and the variety of executives identified with different vested interests, do much to provide checks and balances that put a damper on personal favoritism. This is not a naïve proclamation that blood ties or old school ties are inconsequential. But, generally, they count in opening the original opportunity and maintaining visibility. So, although it does not hurt to be married to the boss's daughter, to get ahead one must be able to produce at least as well as the competition, because there are no longer many bosses around who exercise, or even want to exercise, absolute authority in these matters. On occasion, sympathy was expressed for a junior member of the family of a top executive who might be judged by sterner standards than his peers to prove that favoritism was ruled out. The intense drive exhibited by some executives' family members whom we saw or heard about may well be a reaction to this particular concern. No large corporation can long afford inbreeding at the cost of stagnating its enterprise. The business community is familiar with casualties attributable to stagnating management of previously successful companies. Some of the interviewees were replacements for just such managers. They gave some examples of the financial and investment community's sensitivity to the quality of a company's management and its role as an external monitor of that quality.

4

Educational and Organizational Factors in Development

Purpose of Special Education

In replying to our questions concerning the purpose of special education for upper management, the most common response involved the concept of broadening. In effect this response paralleled the view that one of the prime objectives of development is to prepare managers more adequately for an uncertain future coping with job demands that have not yet been created.[1] This makes it difficult to specify the particular kind of managerial product one wants to develop. However, some observations can be made about what special education is *not* expected to do.

There were no comments about marked changes in personality that had been effected by training. Some executives strongly disavowed any thought that this could be done, being of the opinion that personality patterns were firmly established well before a person went to work and certainly before he reached the executive ranks. The most-often reported reasons for special training at the senior levels involved building strength on strength, not repairing weaknesses, for those with significant weakness usually had been culled and little return was anticipated from additional investment.

[1] E. H. Schein, *Organizational Psychology* (Englewood Cliffs, N.J.: Prentice-Hall, Inc., 1965).

Though not usually thought of as literally part of the job context, broadening was taken in several companies to include increasing participation in coping with the problems of society. This was not restricted to roles in which people represented their employer. Explicit recognition was given to social attitudes and values, which were considered at least partial criteria of organizational effectiveness.

Influence of Special Education on Advancement

"Formal education will be less important in relation to total experience and continuing development as a man approaches the age when top management leadership is in sight." The reader may recall this quotation from F. A. Bond near the beginning of this report. Our interviewees corroborate that finding. Never did a promotee or decision-maker volunteer an observation that a particular training course or educational program was a determining factor in a choice for executive succession. It was only after the interviewer asked if any special educational experience was viewed as influential in the decision-making that comments on the subject were elicited.

That is not to say that some people did not attribute value to certain kinds of educational activity for management personnel in improving the outlook, insights, or performance of top management. Some were strong supporters of such activities. However, they were in no sense considered to be qualification prerequisites for promotion. If they contributed to an individual's accomplishments, all well and good, though a direct connection between curriculum content and performance could seldom be made. It was the job performance that counted in the final analysis.

A particular educational experience comes closer to influencing a promotion decision when it is seen by the decision-makers as resembling the work situation and where performance in that experience can be regarded as a substitute for some equivalent on-the-job performance. Certain conditions are fairly essential to create such a situation. These conditions would include having rather sizable numbers of people from the same company participate in the same course (at the same time, ideally), so that norms could be developed as a basis for making comparative judgments. This condition is infrequently met because it is usually attainable only by a very large or very homogeneous company. Moreover, the company must consider the course to be inherently valid, that is, to closely resemble important components of a real job. It should be sufficiently demanding to bring out the best in those who "have it" and should offer a considerable amount of vigorous intellectual give and take to provide a measure of how an individual makes out in a fast company of peers. This implies that the quality of content and of participants is sufficiently high to pose real challenge. A further condition is that management gets good feedback information from the training course.

It will be noted that these conditions describe something close to a simulation exercise. There has been increasing interest by organizations in experimentation with simulation exercises for screening purposes. However, this type of situation is still exceptional, although approximated by one or two corporations in our sample. Usually, no formal appraisal takes place in the educational setting (outside of regular college courses, it is usually forbidden), and the variety of courses offered to different individuals makes comparison impossible. A course performance that is not outstanding is unlikely to cause disqualification in subsequent promotion actions (people rarely "fail" these courses). However, outstanding school performance may give more visibility to a potential candidate or reinforce an already strong image.

Bear in mind that the promotees with whom we have been involved begin with a visibility and demonstrated competence that antedates their assignment to training. It may be that, as reflected in some interviews, special education courses are more realistically looked upon as exercises to avoid obsolescence than as additions to an already high competence level. Generally, it is the fittest who have survived rugged competition, in which case it may be difficult to ascribe additional increments of effective performance to specific training.

Motivational Implications of Formal Training

Despite the fervently repeated view that all development is fundamentally self-development, initiative in seeking training out of normal work channels has been reported by only a minority of promotees. Those who did take initiative were the few who had a consciously planned approach to career opportunities, as contrasted to the basic task-centeredness of most individuals. In the majority of cases, developmental courses were taken at a superior's suggestion (sometimes prompted by the management development staff). In a number of individuals who worked in companies where some participation in a management training course was the norm, one might detect a note of triumph when they said that they had reached their present status without having attended a course. As previously reported, our respondents tended to associate achievement with performance in operational rather than educational situations, and so they spoke less about the latter.

It is interesting perhaps that the less than anticipated attention to technical implications of development activities was offset in some degree by attention to motivational implications. For instance, "broadening" was not discussed much in terms of specific skills or knowledge added by training. Instead benefits were attributed to what educational experiences had done to increase one's awareness of factors outside of one's own specialty and experience that needed to be taken into account in management problem-solving and decision-making, and in developing motivation to learn more or to gain more experience in these other areas subsequent to the formal training course. Some of these benefits were ascribed to fewer inhibitions when exchanging views with strangers than with people you have to live with, and to having time to sit back and think. Related to this was the comment offered by a promotee that the management course had changed his attitude toward experimentation. He was more willing to try different methods of management and more willing to accept the risks involved when subordinates engaged in experimentation with new ideas.

Another point brought out was that the management course provided opportunities for contacts with people who were successful in other companies and showed that they had problems similar to one's own, so that one came to realize that his own problems were not uniquely attributable to his situation or his inadequacies. That is to say, it was a confidence-building experience. Also, the contacts sometimes proved useful later as resources of information and advice from people who dealt with problems similar to one's own. In addition, selection for high-level training was interpreted as a company testimonial indicating that one was considered to have potential and deserved special treatment reserved for only a few. Here an expression of confidence generated self-confidence.

Early College Education

The college graduate's early area of specialization was emphasized as a factor in his initial selection and as having bearing on his career track, particularly in determining whether or not he would start on a technical route. A major in a technical area may be required as a ticket of admission and "union card," as for example, in manufacturing or research, as well as providing the necessary "language training." However, as entry is gained to the general management ranks, specific technical training diminishes in importance and can be supplied when needed by specialists who report to the general manager.

Among those now in general management who originally embarked upon a career in a special or technical field—a considerable proportion of the interviewees—there was frequent mention of a move toward becoming a generalist after only a brief exposure to work in their specialty or, even earlier, while they were still in college. Accountants, engineers, natural scientists, even research Ph.D.'s are among those included in the group who discovered that their abilities, outlooks, or aspirations did not comfortably fit the occupation around which their college education had been oriented. In most instances, it was not that they did not perform well or were not interested, but rather that they were more interested in other things, such as working with people, organizing activities, coping with management problems, exerting power, seeing their work produce results. The origin of these interests and related competencies very often could be traced to influences outside the classroom, including organized or informal extracurricular activity as well as community, family, and childhood background.

Because the rewards for achievement early in the work history of college graduates are more often geared to technical achievement than to management-related abilities, a company may lose or lose sight of valuable executive potential if it chiefly depends upon these specialists to make their general abilities known. The opportunity to do so is not always evident, nor is the desire to do so always fostered by immediate work demands and the local managerial climate.

The question arises as to whether college education, particularly in schools of business, might be modified to help students gain more insight and better anticipate the organizational dynamics of which they will become a part, including the influences upon career growth that are pointed out in this study.

Organization Policy

Policies and procedures for personnel development need to be established and modified to anticipate changing conditions. This is axiomatic. Similarly, the programs need to be integrated with other operating management decisions. Too often personnel development plans lag behind, to be patched together at moments of crisis. Changes in the nature of the business have to be reflected in changes in the management development program if the program is not to result in the selection and training of people to fight the last competitive war instead of the next one.

The nature of the executive development program, of course, depends upon the stage of the corporation's general development and the basic policies that govern it. For example, an organization that is relatively new or is experiencing very rapid growth is unlikely to be able to meet its requirements for growth with the executive talent within its own ranks. Later on, as conditions become more stable, steps can be taken to foster internal growth to meet a larger part of its requirements.

It must be recognized also that within the dynamic flux of competitive enterprise the criteria of organizational and individual success are multiple, with varying priorities for different organizational units at different times. When focus shifts and is blurred, confusion appears because all criteria are considered more or less equally and simultaneously relevant. Then, as indicated in the survey reported by Lawler, we have the unrealistic situation where unrewarding arguments arise because of attitudes suggesting that "the good manager needs to possess every human virtue" and because of "very little agreement about what comprised effective performance."[2]

What are some of the questions asked that reveal what kind of management development policies need to be established? The questions obviously have more generality than the answers, which are conditioned by the aims, objectives, and circumstances of separate enterprises. We will deal with some of the more outstanding illustrations, provided by our recent interview experience, of problem situations in the decision-making process.

[2] M. D. Dunnette, *et al., op. cit.*

Personnel Flow and Mix

One question is, What should be the design of personnel flow through the management development system? Collateral questions include: What is the foreseeable requirement for senior executives five years, ten years, and further ahead? What is the desirable age-range and experience prerequisite to assuming such duties? What is the breakdown of supply and demand for the original pool of career executive potentials, and at each echelon and in each of the experience areas through which developing executives pass? What has been the company's past experience and what are its forecasts for turnover, attrition, and selection ratios in promotions at these several points, and what is considered desirable? What do the facts and policy decisions derived from the foregoing tell us about changes required in recruitment, selection, placement, company organization, training and education, compensation and retirement?

Policy on the mix of people that ought to make up a particular management group is never defined in formal terms. The operational policy takes shape as a cumulative effect of individual decisions. Thus, if Number One in a division has generated a number of innovations, it may be considered appropriate to appoint as Number Two man, and probable successor, a person who is strong in management skills, and who can concentrate more upon consolidating the organizational effort. Or an appointment is made after a turbulent period of corporate reorganization when a calming hand rather than a brilliant mind was needed. Or, if among the executives appointed to the division in the past few years outsiders predominate, it may be time to balance off with a person who has come up through the division, in order to strengthen the technical input of the top level and to improve communication with, and the motivational climate for, subordinate echelons. At one time it may be deemed best to bring together matching personalities, whereas at another time it is felt that assignment of complementary or contrasting personalities is needed to give the organization a certain tone. Similarly, the purpose of a given appointment may be to reduce technical homogeneity in a group, as expressed by such statements as "retailing is run too much by retailers" or "finance is too important to be left to accountants."

The changing nature of the industry is quite often reflected in the changing abilities needed, so that the leaders in the petroleum industry who could physically beat their competitors have given way to the systems analysts, scientists, and engineers who understand the working of thoroughly integrated industrial systems.

These requirements for mix do not appear in position descriptions. Failure to offer decision-makers information relevant to considerations of this sort can discredit the work of the management development staff. This was illustrated by the complaint of a vice-president that he was offered a list of ordinary prospects for promotion, replete with pages of routine data, but lacking in just those critical bits essential to differentiate among the people listed in terms of the particular *situation* to be occupied.

It is not likely that this kind of information requirement will be met by any form of memorandum communication. The complaint is symptomatic of a more fundamental communication deficiency that exists so long as a pattern of close and continuing interaction is lacking between those in operating management and those conducting executive development systems.

Stability Versus Change

What value does the company or an organizational unit place upon stability and maturity versus vitality and innovation (allowing that this is a somewhat artificial dichotomy)?

To answer this question a number of issues have to be faced, as is reflected in this sampling. You cannot have it both ways. Judgments as to trade-offs need to be made, aiming to optimize over-all organizational effectiveness. There needs to be a " 'creative tension' between stability or security on the one hand and sources of disruption or challenge on the other."[3]

If youth is to be served through intensive development and rapid advancement, and this involves a change in pace for the organization, hard facts of life have to be resolved. Unless opportunities exist for younger people to move up, incentives for them are devalued. There is a risk that they may age in the job, that their prospective successors will also age in their jobs, and that the management ranks will become progressively more homogeneous in age and outlook. If the youth movement was designed to favor a climate for organizational change, the chances of realizing that purpose are lessened as the development pipelines clog up.

What should be the policies toward those who have given years of faithful service or toward those whose achievements flatten out at a level below the one they aspired to and the one the company expected? Is the organization prepared to consider the costs of early retirement or executive featherbedding as part of the normal costs of business in order to keep open the channels of growth, development, and advancement? Is the company prepared to pay the toll of personal casualties induced by attendant stresses?

If stability and maturity are to be given premium values in order to increase assurance that management decisions will be in experienced hands and to guard against errors of impetuosity and inexperience, another set of problems must be met. What does this policy do to the internal and external company image? Can an atmosphere of challenge be supported to attract and retain bright, achievement-oriented people and to infuse new ideas? One company operated on the assumption that there is a tendency for an individual to recycle his old ideas every five years if he stays in the same job.

Affecting the adoption or implementation of one or the other of these policy alternatives, of course, are different circumstances

[3] Donald C. Pelz, "Creative Tensions in the Research and Development Climate," *Science*, CLVII (July 14, 1967), pp. 160–165.

of organizational life. Periods of economic growth, company expansion, diversification, and technological change favor youth and innovation. Periods in which opposite trends are at work favor stability and maturity.

Mobility

Cutting across considerations involved in these last few paragraphs are questions about the extent to which rotation and mobility ought to be made part of the management development program, and at what stage. Companies introduce rotation at various points. Some start a new college graduate on the rounds during his first year to get acquainted with a variety of operations. Others wait until a person is clearly in the running for a place in the top corporate hierarchy. In most organizations rotation is instituted somewhere in the middle management ranks.

Experience and research generally affirm the proposition that greater mobility of managers increases the range of choice and flexibility in deployment of human resources and most often results in a more adaptable organization. It has been suggested that mobility contributes to unfreezing old outlooks by removing the supports for them that are rooted in a specific situation.[4] It may be that the individual who comes into a new situation with high personal status is less burdened with the status quo and so is more potent as an innovator. Illustrating the other side is the frequent experience of those who go away for a time to participate in management training and then, upon returning to their old situation, find that the new learning is difficult to implement because the trainee is the only one who sees the situation differently and who is motivated to change it. Mobility is costly, in any case. Each position change sets off a chain reaction. The higher the position the longer the chain. The more frequent the changes, the greater the cost. Economic criteria do apply.

[4] K. Lewin, "Frontiers in Group Dynamics: Concept, Method and Reality in Social Science," *Human Relations*, I, 1 (1947), pp. 5–42.

We have already pointed out that a balance has to be struck between the conflicting interests of corporate management and subordinate unit management. The conflicts imposed between corporate and individual welfare are also well known. How often is it fair to ask a man to move and to endure the inconveniences and stresses of physical and psychological reacclimatization, not only for himself but for his family? Are these strains relevant and valid tests of the prospective executive's survival probability in the top management arena? Or do they reduce personal effectiveness and waste good potential?

Our observations would suggest that opportunity knocks less often at the door of one who waits than for those who are holding the door open. We heard about a good number of instances where opportunity has fallen to the one among several persons who was willing to claim it by moving. The larger the organization and the more widespread its activities the more this is true—and large organizations are tending to predominate and their national and international activities are tending to increase. One illustration is the case of an individual who accepted a foreign assignment after three others had turned it down and who performed notably well. He and those who spoke about him agreed that this marked a point of departure for a subsequent rapid rise.

The operational facts are more in evidence than the management policies that match them. Hence, there is reason to believe that an increasing obligation is going to be put upon corporate policy-makers to examine these questions more closely, develop more information about them, and to make clear the policy bearing upon them in the interest of good business management. Problems relating to Americans working in company operations in foreign cultures, and to executives of other nationalities in American-owned firms, illustrate this particularly well.

Emotional Factors in Decision-Making

It was obvious here, as others have also recognized, that

decision-makers are subjected to much stress in the making of people-centered decisions, and that the emotional issues involved tend to be kept under cover because it is felt that only rational matters should influence business decisions and policy. Yet suppressed or repressed emotions have their impact upon how policy is made and carried out.[5] For example, one could examine the influence of guilt feelings on decision-making that affects executives. This might include such things as guilt feelings of decision-makers for having put a man in a position for which he proves unsatisfactory. It might also include situations where the removal of a man would obviously cause great psychological distress and material loss to the individual concerned. Also, there are situations where procrastination in dealing with an individual's ineffective performance has encouraged his presumption of a satisfactory performance.

Some further questions that arise have not been answered yet: How often are weak compromises offered as palliatives because decision-makers cannot cope with the complexity of their own motivations toward others rather than because of the objective complexity of the problem itself? How do the research findings with regard to individual versus group risk-taking apply to decisions on management succession? Are more high-risk, high-gain decisions on selection of individuals for top management positions likely to be taken by group rather than by individual decision-makers? Is action on the removal of an unsatisfactory executive more likely to be taken by a group rather than an individual decision-maker?

Rational decision-making has long been held up as an American ideal. Carried to an extreme, this ideal can induce a false sense of security behind porous psychological defenses, if it ignores the true relevance and impact of emotional factors in the formulation of policies and decisions.

---

[5] Chris Argyris, *Interpersonal Competence and Organizational Effectiveness* (Homewood, Ill.: Dorsey Press—Richard D. Irwin, 1962).

Development Program Management

Whatever the structure of the system, naturally, the functioning of the process of top management development and succession and the success with which it operates is determined to a considerable measure by how it is managed. The policies and machinery that govern the system and keep it in motion cannot, however, be set apart for examination. They are component parts of the total system. Thus, in our earlier commentary we have had to dovetail aspects of policy and machinery. But for convenience of exposition it is necessary at this point to lift out certain components for separate examination.

The vigor of the management development and succession system is proportional to the extent of involvement and support demonstrated by top corporate officialdom. To be sure, a good system is not thus automatically assured. But without such support and involvement, the best conceived programs will be more form than substance.

We will not undertake to estimate what degree of involvement of top executives in management resource development as compared to other elements in the corporate structure will optimize the total system. Some chief executives said that theirs is more a personnel job than anything else. In any case, no two systems are likely to fit the same equation.

Top Level Support and Involvement

We can testify to what is already known: the range of top level support and involvement varies widely. At one end of the spectrum is the situation where the chief executive officer meets every Tuesday afternoon with a designated group to review, plan, and make decisions about executive development and appointments. At the other end we find the chief executive who involves himself only intermittently or superficially, or only in a few critical cases, or at moments of crisis. A familiar observation is that management development is often least accepted where it is most needed since aggressive development of managers can be a threat to the security of the limited man who is in an executive position. A high degree of top level support and involvement will usually be reflected in a highly structured system of planning, review, appraisal, and decision-making, with consistent time involvement at all management levels. Low support and involvement will be reflected in a more unpredictable pattern of case-by-case decisions under pressure of immediate urgencies with more erratic variations of involvement from unit to unit and from time to time.

Reinforcement theory will be well demonstrated in these circumstances. Where the boss is interested in management development, spends his time and money at it, and requires subordinate echelons to show reports and results, most everyone plays ball. When the boss does not show that he cares, the number of quixotic executives taking their time from "more important things" will be few.

In general, the developing of subordinates is taken seriously as a responsibility by top management. Exhortations by chief executives that their managers give serious attention to this responsibility are frequent. But exhortation is not enough. This responsibility comes to be taken seriously where it is made obvious through repeated critical decisions that the manager who is disposed to do it all himself, instead of teaching others to do it, may lose out in the race for advancement. In this way, it is shown that the person who absorbs himself mainly with technical details in his management area risks being tagged as a specialist who is too narrow-gauged to be assigned more general management duties. Or he may make himself irreplaceable where he is because he has developed no replacements.

Personnel and Development Organization

In some places, the function of development or training of managers is part of the mission of the personnel department; in other places, these functions will be found in separate organizational units.

Those in favor of a single management hold that, since it is agreed that the two functions need to be thoroughly integrated, over-all objectives are most efficiently attained by having one person in charge. The proponents of the opposing point of view contend that in a single department, training and development requirements tend to be subordinated. They say: an extra layer of management tends to impede communication with top management and reduces responsiveness to and by the management developers; the personnel director is usually too busy to take adequate notice of the special needs of the development program; attention and emphasis is given to the more immediately urgent demands of day-to-day operations at the sacrifice of development goals that take longer to realize; and the education and experience of most personnel men is deficient in the training and development field.

Top management is called upon to decide how these viewpoints are to be accommodated and to minimize the frictions between them.

Executive Development Program Management

The status, influence, and power of the staff responsible for managing the executive development and succession system can be expected to be commensurate with the importance attributed to its function in the office of the chief executive and in the board room. Where the program director is close to the chief executive, personally, physically, and on the organization chart, he will be a person of considerable power. As the number of links increases between him and the chief executive, his influence diminishes.

Though it would be unusual to find the program director with any direct executive power in the making of choices for succession, we have a case here where knowledge is power—knowledge about the people, the organization, and the system. The individual who accumulates this information and governs its analysis, evaluation, and dissemination is a person to be reckoned with by all whose destinies he may affect. Where close rapport and confidence has been established between the senior executives and the development staff the former tend toward a heavy dependence upon the information and judgments of the latter. This is not an unmixed blessing.

It is hard to sustain the role of "honest broker," in fact as well as in appearance, to those outside of the inner circle. It requires no end of sensitivity to the needs and attitudes of all parties involved, as well as a clear and continuous discernment of the staff man's proper role. The judicious exercise of the influence that can reside in this staff capacity, located at the turbulent confluence of organizational forces, requires a sense of balance crucial to the exercise of a higher order of diplomacy. The typical management development officer, who thinks of himself as an agent essential in a change process but not himself altered by it, can aptly be described as a catalyst. If he falls prey to temptation or pressure to extend his influence to advance or hinder the cause of key individuals in order to affect operational consequences outside of his legitimate sphere of influence, he risks becoming caught up in the snares of corporate politics. This can happen even if he only leaves this impression because he failed to deliberately guard against it. Under such circumstances, his power resides in his alliances. Lacking any operational power base, changes in the senior executive ranks may exert radical leverage upon the strength of his position. The criteria of survival may then supplant the criteria of service as guides to his behavior, whereupon the risk that he will be identified as personally self-serving and his staff activity as self-perpetuating increases. Naturally, the operational effectiveness of the management development effort is quickly eroded in these circumstances.

From contacts with a number of interviewees and development officials, an impression is created that the part of the latter's function that involves person-to-person counseling is generally well accepted. This role involves bringing to the attention of decision-makers information about individuals that they may not have, creating awareness of prospects in other parts of the company, identifying people who may be missed because they are thought to be confined to a given area of interest or ability, mediating among units competing for the same man, and helping prospects to learn about opportunities and to assess their own capabilities and development needs. When interviewees talked about these situations, they made favorable references to the names of the persons who were helpful. Unfortunately, however, these counseling contributions are often offset by disaffection with the routine forms and procedures of input and output, and these are identified by the users as *the* management development system.

It is ironic that one finds instances in the interviews when, in response to a question about the usefulness of the management development system, one receives responses such as "it does not exist" or "it makes a lot of extra paper work." Yet at the same time, the same person may make reference to information used, advice received, or discussions held in particular instances that would not have been available were it not for the operations of the development staff. It seems that sometimes the development staff succeeds in its objective of helping without being personally obtrusive, only to suffer the indignity of being judged by reactions to their more visible operational instruments.

Another set of factors affecting the role of the executive development staff as they perceive it and play it, and as it is perceived by their high-ranking clients, stems from certain determining characteristics of the situation in which they must operate.

At the beginning of this report we attempted to describe the perspective from the executive suite and we said that we expected the people close at hand to loom largest and those further down the line to be less visible. By contrast, in the broadside view of the personnel administrators, individuals at the different hierarchical levels, while having different status values, are of more or less the same apparent size and visibility. Their involvement with the people at the various levels is more nearly equal. In the pyramidal organization structure there are more people near the base than near the apex. Hence, a correspondingly larger portion of the personnel man's time and attention is likely to be devoted to the larger categories. This, coupled with the fact that the operational influence of personnel officials is usually less at the higher levels than at the lower levels, may lead higher executives to see a contrast between what is important to them and what the personnelists are working at most of the time. Maybe this, in part, accounts for the widespread attitude among executives that the management development system bedevils them with procedural trivia in which they discern little of immediate or practical benefit. Then, too, the personnelists are often caught in the middle between the demands of top management and the subjects of the development program, each side anxious that its interests be guarded and its views properly communicated to the other.

How, then, can the management development managers be helped to establish the conditions that permit them to practice neutrality among the contending forces they serve, yet be perceived as benevolently inclined by each of the forces? The answer to this question deserves a study of its own. We think it important, as we approach this study's end, to highlight, by reference to this incomplete assortment of problems, some of the possible effects of executive development program management upon the people who are subject to it and served by it.

5

Plan for a Research Program

Management Development Research Issues

Management development is not a separate entity or process. Because we give it a name, a place on the organization chart, and write a book about it, we are inclined to treat it as a separate component of management with a set of rules all its own.

Management *development* is not a researchable area when extracted from its context. That context is *management*. The conceptual basis and setting for study needs to be the totality of management, its systems and processes. Within this framework, development can be looked upon as a component or as a variable related to other variables in the management process equation. Too long and too often this variable has been treated as an unknown. This perhaps reflects a philosophy of despair—that the very complicated characteristics and behavioral principles of management development are for all practical purposes unknowable.

Compounding the difficulty of systematic study of management development has been the protective curtain woven around the executive precincts, which insures not only that the variables are unknowable but also that as subjects of study these people are untouchable. Fortunately, ours is but one of a number of research efforts that demonstrate that this is not necessarily so.

However, as Dunnette and associates conclude from their recent survey for the Richardson Foundation, although training and development of management level employees involve one of the major investments of financial resources that organizations make and managers consistently stress their interest in research on training and development, very few organizations are doing any.[1] Hence, there is practically no solid information available with which to evaluate the effectiveness of present methods of development or how much return to the organization is obtained from these investments. This neglect of research by corporations themselves may explain why management, under pressure to cope with the complexities of human motivation, abilities, and behavior, has been notably vulnerable to fads and gimmicks in training operations. Nor has painful exposure to panaceas effected immunization against reinfection by another enthusiasm with the next appealingly simple idea.

"The major issue . . . is to recognize that we are still primarily talking about an art rather than the making of scientific statements. . . . Very few studies have systematically evaluated the impact of these different practices. To the extent this continues, management development will continue to be an art rather than a science or an applied technology."[2] These observations by Dr. Seymour Levy of Pillsbury Company about an earlier survey to establish principles of effective management development are timely and accurate.

To make the variable of management development less of an unknown requires, first, that more be learned of its characteristics. How do we describe it? Second, it requires that research be done to establish principles that govern the management development component in the over-all management system. How does it work? What contributes to it working well or poorly? How can it be made to work better?

The present exploratory study has been principally addressed

---

[1] M. D. Dunnette, *et al., op. cit.,* pp. 44–60.

[2] S. Levy in his review of W. S. Wikstron, *Developing Managerial Competence: Changing Concepts, Emerging Practices* (Studies in Personnel Policy No. 189, National Industrial Conference Board, 1964), in *Personnel Psychology,* XVIII, 1 (1965), p. 127.

to the first of the two phases. We have tried to examine the characteristics of present programs through the eyes of the principals who direct, control, and are subject to them. From their operating experiences we have generated some ideas and concepts included in the preceding text to stimulate thought, particularly with regard to researchable questions. Lack of reference groups against which our "successful" group could be compared did not permit us to go further. If we go no further, if the second phase of systematic research on these questions is not conducted, we have only taken one more step on a treadmill, and the echoes of conventional management wisdom will continue to reverberate from generation to generation.

As was said at the start, we could not expect to come up with *the* answers, only places and ways to look for them. Despite the effort to tie generalizations to specific incidents reported by the interviewees, it is difficult to assess whether the wisdom displayed here, or some parts of it, is more or less than conventional. As there are no norms available, we will have to suspend that judgment, recognizing that one man's innovation is another's old hat, and that these constructs and interpretations are drawn from material given by men, at present established in rather powerful positions of management, who have been conditioned by the management thinking and practice existing during their careers. Of course, to the extent that the men in this sample are representative, there can be nothing here that is completely new to managers of similar organizations and responsibilities.

Nonetheless, it is felt that the raw material does provide a basis for further research. We will not again catalog here the large number of research questions that can be asked but will instead offer an over-all research plan that can embrace a large proportion of them.

Assumptions

First, let us state a few fundamental assumptions upon which this presentation is conditioned:

1. In management development and succession the ability of executives to make sound decisions is rarely in question. The main problem is to get enough reliable information to act upon.

2. Managers can point to people they consider to be promising executive material.

3. The cumulative processes culminating in a person being chosen for a senior executive position cover an extended time period, often reaching back to an early point in his career. Research should therefore cover a sufficient time span to provide information on a relevant sequence of actions, events, and decisions.

4. Business operates in a condition of continuous change and the object of management activity is almost always to induce individual, group, or systems change. Management development involves changes in the individuals concerned, changes in the relations among individuals, changes in the organizations of which they are a part, and interactions among the changes affecting individuals, groups, and organizations. Hence, a comprehensive study of management development processes and succession decisions should include individual, group, and organizational differences and changes as well as the interactions among these over time.

5. Statistical comparisons and/or research controls are essential to establishing generalizable findings in the field of management development.

6. There are discoverable differences in individuals, groups, organizations, and processes that are associated with differences in effectiveness of management development as defined by criteria of individual and organizational gain.

7. Future-oriented longitudinal research programs of considerable scope have been lacking and are needed. Because the variety of research questions that can be profitably examined is great, it is not likely that an all-at-once research design would be practical to implement. Therefore, to make for the greatest generality and applicability of findings it is

essential to have a consistent framework or model that can incorporate component projects of a continuing research program.
8. Our final assumption is that management will support meaningful research in management development.

Proposed Plan

Starting with the present, the first aim of the research plan would be to determine what differences exist in the characteristics of those considered to have high potential as top executives (HI) from those not so identified (NOT). This can be done for one large company or organizational unit, or for a group of companies or organizational units, as follows:

A. Ask the top management echelon and several subordinate management levels to identify, at any level subordinate to them, those individuals whom they consider to have a high probability of rising to a stipulated level of top management. Example: "List the names of all persons in the company, of any age or experience, whom you think have a 75 per cent chance of some day becoming a vice-president." The levels and percentages could be adjusted to be appropriate to the level of the nominating managers and nominees involved. (It is also possible to include nominations from peer and subordinate levels. To simplify further exposition, we will not do so.)

B. For each nominee, select from personnel files one person (or more, if needed to meet statistical requirements of a specific project) who matches the nominee in age and current position echelon. Matching on additional control variables may be considered, but it should be kept in mind that the more variables that are included in equating the HI and NOT groups, the less the number of variables that are free to vary in subsequent comparative analyses. Where the numbers of NOT's available to match a HI is greater than required, a random selection procedure would be used to prevent sampling bias.

C. Establish a set of variables including characteristics for which relevant information is available or could be obtained for individuals in both groups. The four major categories of information are indicated below with examples of each category.

1. Individual:
   Age.
   Intelligence.
   Performance ratings.
   Interests.
   Attitudes.

2. Group:
   Number in unit.
   Member's rank in unit on peer rating of esteem.
   Average tenure of employees in unit.
   Time members are engaged in solo activities/Time in group activities.
   Average job satisfaction level.

3. Developmental-educational-training:
   Highest degree obtained.
   Number of management training courses taken in last five years.
   Current salary/Salary five years ago.
   Self-report of level of management aspiration.
   Need-achievement score.

4. Organizational-situational:
   Immediate superior's time in position.
   Unit earnings/Investment (relative to other corporate units during past three years).
   Measure of autonomy versus control in organizational climate.

Number of significant reorganizations involving unit in past ten years.

New products developed in past five years/Total number of products currently marketed.

In this design all four types of characteristics are ultimately associated with an individual. Thus, for example, an individual may be identified in part as one who is 40 years old, in the company ten years, in his present position five years, working in a unit of twenty people, with three immediate subordinates, in a staff capacity, for a 60-year-old superior who is nondirective, in a field location, in a subsidiary corporation that lost money last year.

D. A number of comparative analyses could then be made, illustrated by the following questions:

To deal with the *present* first:

1. Over-all, what characteristics significantly differentiate between HI and NOT groups?

2. Are the characteristics that differentiate between the HI and NOT groups the same regardless of the management echelon providing HI nominations?

3. To what extent is there overlap of nominees listed by the several management levels? At what hierarchical levels in the organization do appreciable numbers of HI's (for example, 25 per cent of total nominations at a given level) first become visible to top echelon management? To the other echelons of management?

Looking to the *future* these further questions can be posed:

4. In Y years, what are the respective rates of advance of those originally in the HI and NOT groups?

5. Do the characteristics that originally differentiated between HI and NOT groups also predict subsequent advancement? In other words, will those having the most differentiating characteristics favoring the HI's move

ahead significantly faster than those more like the NOT's?

6. At time Y, are there other differences that have emerged distinguishing HI's and NOT's, such as rates of retirement, illness, turnover, discharge, and resignation?

7. What is the earliest level at which nominations of HI's are sufficiently reliable and predictive of future attainment of vice-presidential (or other high) level to provide a useful basis for organizational planning and a guide to individual development?

8. Are there characteristics of individuals and their developmental histories, available at a junior level, that are useful in determining characteristics of situations and organizations for which they are most likely to be suitable at a senior level, and which, among alternative routes, are likely to contribute most to required development?

9. If the present analyses are repeated at time Y, will the same characteristics differentiate HI's and NOT's?

10. With original age and position level constant, over Y years, do HI's originally nominated by the more senior management levels move up more rapidly than those nominated by lower levels?

11. At time Y, are the original HI nominees more likely to be closely associated with their nominators than with others of status equal to the nominators?

This model is also designed to take into account *changes between present and future*. These may be "natural" changes that impinge upon some groups and not upon others, so that a basis of comparison could be established. A question might be:

12. Are differences that have occurred in growth rates of companies originally sampled being accompanied by differential effects upon aspects of management devel-

opment? The continuing availability of data from "before" permits more meaningful interpretations to be made of these effects than is usually the case where only "after" the fact data is available.

These may be "experimental" changes that have been deliberately introduced. Because the research questions and design can be more nearly custom-made and the experimental inputs better controlled and measured, findings are likely to be clearer than for natural experiments. Here are some examples of research that fall in this category:

13. An hypothesis is advanced that because of the rapid rate of advancement necessary in relatively few years to develop a high-potential young individual to assume corporate executive responsibility, it would be advantageous to institute a program in which a select group would be advanced two echelons at a time instead of the usual one, thus permitting more time to be spent in a smaller number of positions with the increased average time-in-job offsetting the experience "skipped." By instituting a control so that among a group of HI's, comparable people were assigned to the one-at-a-time and two-at-a-time development schedules, before-and-after comparisons could be made, as well as analysis of the characteristics that distinguished those who performed more satisfactorily from those who performed less satisfactorily in each of the two groups.

14. Comparisons of a similar kind might be made to examine the effects upon management development of instituting a decentralized organization structure, or to determine the different kinds of managers and management development activities that contribute most to operations in decentralized as against centralized structures.

15. Or one might examine the question raised earlier in the

report as to whether individuals who have been given a rather extensive management training course do better if they are then assigned to an organizational unit other than the one from which they came, rather than back to the original unit.

This assortment of fifteen possible studies is only a sparse sampling of the host of possibilities open to research. If one agrees with the statement of Dr. Schein, cited at the outset, that "existing methods are not providing the talent which is needed at higher levels of industry" and that "we continue to lack clear-cut formulations about the process by which such development occurs," then we would suggest that such formulations will not be found in more summaries of what schools and businesses are doing about management development; nor in more *post hoc* testimonials of virtues attributed to various types of development activities; nor in more consumer surveys of likes and dislikes regarding education, training and development policies, procedures, or courses. We would suggest that the time has come to supplant these with systematic research in operational contexts of sufficient scope, with adequate control, over sufficient time, and within a consistent conceptual framework to provide reliable, practically meaningful findings that are translatable into effective management decisions and courses of action.

One might reflect that continuation of the methods of study that have become conventional in management development is likely to continue to beget conventional management wisdom. Innovative applications of research have to come before innovative findings.

The plan for a management development research program presented here is offered as an illustration of one possible approach —not the only approach—that can be accomplished with the collaboration of organizations like those that participated in this exploratory phase. Given the kind of support demonstrated by these organizations, we believe that such research can be carried out with useful results. There would appear to be justification now to give such a program the priority, time, and energy commensurate with the magnitude of the investment that industry has in its managers and in its programs for their development.

Outline of Topics Covered in Interviews

PROMOTEE INTERVIEWS

A. *The Position*
  1. Personal abilities, characteristics, or requirements to perform this job? Relative weight?
     a. Which of these are unique to the position, company, industry, geography?
     b. How did Promotee (P) learn of these requirements?
  2. Do requirements differ from previous job?
     a. How did P come to have these "new" abilities?
  3. Did the decision-makers have the same requirements in mind? Does P know?
  4. What sources of information does P think Decision-Makers (DM's) used in assessing qualifications?
     a. How does P think the decision was made?
B. *Experience*
  1. Something in P's career that particularly helped develop any of these qualities?
     a. How did it help?
     b. How was it later used?
  2. Additional incidents?
  3. A time in P's career when a specific situation arose in the company or industry that particularly influenced his development?
     a. The jobs he was assigned at this point?
     b. How did it affect his development? What results?
  4. A time in P's career when he was given a particular assignment to help development, but which had little effect on his performance?

       a. What was the assignment? Why no effect?

    5. To what extent was P's development planned or fortuitous?

C. *The Decision*

    1. Who does P think had a part in the decision?

       a. Actual final decision?

       b. Advisory role?

       c. Supplied relevant information?

    2. How long has P known the DM(s)?

       a. Relationship to him (them)?

       b. Specific contributions to P's development?

    3. P became aware of being considered for the position when and how?

    4. Did P want or seek it? Did he do anything about it?

    5. Factors that put P in the running for the position?

       a. Long period of planned assignments?

       b. Outstanding performance over time?

       c. Outstanding performance on specific assignment?

       d. Specialized qualifications or training?

       e. Formal management inventory procedures?

       f. Seniority for position?

       g. Personal connections?

    6. Abilities P wishes were stronger for this job?

       a. Others' efforts to help with them?

       b. P's specific plans to develop them?

    7. P's other plans for future development?

DECISION-MAKER INTERVIEWS

A. *The Position Itself*

    1. How did vacancy arise? (new position, retirement, promotion)

    2. How long had the position existed?

    3. How far in advance was the need to fill the vacancy known?

    4. Was the job changed in any way when P was assigned? Why?

    5. How was it determined that P was qualified for the job?

6. Personal abilities, characteristics, or requirements to perform this job? Relative weight of each?

   a. Which are unique to the position, industry, company, geography?

7. How was it known that the job required these particular abilities?

   a. Trouble because someone lacked one or more?

   b. Was anyone else involved in determining requirements?

   c. Were these requirements put in writing somewhere?

8. How do requirements of this job differ from previous job?

   a. How did he come to have the new abilities?

B. *The Man P Himself*

1. How long known to Decision-Maker (DM)?

   a. P as a "comer"? When?

   b. How did DM spot his potential?

   c. Did DM take any specific action at this point?

2. How long in advance of appointment was decision reached?

   a. Any action to prepare him?

3. What evidence did DM have that P had each job requirement?

   a. What sources did DM draw on to learn about P?

4. Was P not as strong in any of these characteristics as ideally desired?

   a. Was anything specific done to help P to become stronger in each of these areas?

   b. If so, how did it work out? What evidence?

5. Was anything done to help P become even stronger in areas of his strength?

   a. How did it work out? What evidence?

6. Something in his experience that particularly helped in the development of one of his skills?

7. Incidents for other skill development?

8. Some specific condition that helped his development or affected his selection?

   a. How did condition operate?

      b. What evidence it made a difference?

       (for example: in good market; on ground floor of new development)

   9. Was P given a particular task, or assignment, or opportunity to aid his development, but which seemed to have little effect on his performance? Evidence?

C. *Other Aspects of Decision*

   1. Who was involved in the decision-making?

   2. How did they contribute?

   3. Others seriously considered for the job? (inside and outside company)

   4. Compare these men.

   5. Other factors affecting the decision?

D. *Future*

   1. Development activities planned to help P be more effective?

      a. In his present job?

      b. For some future position?

   2. Evidence as to how well he is meeting the job requirements?

Memorandum of Comment, Reservation, or Dissent

Page xi, by DONALD C. STONE:

This is a most constructive report and I am glad it is being published. It should help stimulate more systematic attention to the all-important problem in any organization, namely, of finding and developing the best talent for executive posts. I also found the report very readable.

In reviewing the draft, I thought especially of the applicability of its proposals to government, universities, and voluntary service organizations. These have lagged far behind the better-managed business corporations in providing for executive leadership. The federal government has made great progress in methods of appointment to top positions, and in training and promotion. But a current effort to identify a few persons outstanding in their managerial competences and capable of developing new management applications in new fields revealed only a handful of prospects. The present system does not appear to produce many or provide a ready means for detecting them.

Few state and city governments have made any progress in organizing a system for selecting, rotating, and promoting executive personnel throughout the service. Persons get promoted in the best-administered systems on the basis of ascertained competence, but this is almost entirely restricted to movement within departments— public works, welfare, police, finance, and so on.

Universities have only recently discovered that there is such a field as management. Development and adoption of formal methods of identifying potentiality for positions of department heads, deans, vice-presidents, and presidents is only on the horizon.

In addition to the same reasons why more companies do not do a better job in selecting and developing top executives, government and universities lack the undergirding stimulation and support of first-rate schools of public administration. Legislative bodies in government and faculty processes in universities are a deterrent. Professional associations related to the public service and education have not focused on the top positions. Administrative research has lagged.

Thus, I hope the report on Top Management Development and Succession will get widespread distribution in governmental, university, and other nonprofit organizational circles. CED's Committee on the Improvement of Management in Government should be able to help in putting it in the hands of officials who would most benefit.

Although at first I thought the small sample of business firms would be a very limiting factor in the validity of the report, I found that it provided enough of a "coatrack" on which to hang the discussion. I suppose the sample covered especially well-managed establishments so that the findings would be even more relevant to the run-of-mine companies.

The interpretive highlights are well stated and of course form the guts of the report. My experience in government supports the thesis that the performance of the man to a greater or lesser extent determines the classification of the position. The more elbowroom for initiative and individual style of operation, the more this is true. Especially in positions of "assistant to" and similar individual assignments, it is the man who classifies the job by his performance and not the reverse.

Fast promotion up the ranks of especially gifted talent is necessary not only to have time to get to the top, but also to maximize experience. Payoffs in new experience in most posts run downhill faster after two or three years as contrasted with new posts, not that persons should move that fast.

The heart of the problem is how to make potential talent visible. A companion problem is isolating the distinguishing characteristics of talent. The need for research is especially apparent here. The Research Program Plan in Chapter 5 would no doubt encompass this, and looks like a good one.

A simple practice which every executive can use for limited purposes is to maintain a "Hot Prospect" file. Whenever I see a very superior person who appears to have high potential, I make a note about him and put it in my Hot Prospects file. I was able to put my hands quickly on a considerable number of persons in this way when I moved into the Bureau of the Budget and later in the Economic Cooperation Administration. A considerable number of these persons now occupy strategic positions in the government.

There is a mighty lot of unmined managerial talent hidden away in any organization that has recruited competent persons at lower levels. Many persons never have an opportunity to discover that they have managerial ability, or to demonstrate it. There are so many examples of first-class performance by persons who have never been thought of as administrators but by sheer accident were thrown into a managerial situation and did well, that we know there must be many such persons. I do not know what you can do about this, but it is a great challenge.

I am glad the report points out the problem of the difficulty of the staff man moving into executive channels. It further illustrates this point of hidden talent. I suspect there is even more prejudice or false assumption in government than in business about the unsuitability of a staff person in planning, budgeting, personnel, and so on, for executive positions in the line. My observation is that on the whole they have done remarkably well—better than those who came up from operations—when given the chance. How can their potential be identified and demonstrated?

Index

A

Advances in Social Psychology, 36n

Age
and management development, 8, 29, 30
and management selection, 10, 24, 32, 56–57, 71

AIR. *See* American Institutes for Research.

American Institutes for Research, 2–9

Argyris, Chris, 59n

B

Baxter, Brent, 6n

Berkowitz, L., 36n

"Big fish in the little pond" principle, 41

Boards, Managers, and Company Success, 36n

Bond, F. A., 2n, 48

"Business Bridges to the Campus," 17n

Business schools, 2

C

Campbell, J. P., 2n

Capital resources allocation, 1

Career development. *See* Career planning; Management development.

Career planning, 19, 20

College graduates, attitudes toward big business among, 16–17

Committee for Economic Development, 2
Business-Education Committee of, 2, 3

Communication
between top managers, 8, 13
of performance-rating information, 21–22

Competition for top management positions, 16
Computerization, 17
"Contingency Model of Leadership Effectiveness, A," 36n
Corporation-centered orientation, 28–29
Corporations
in management development study, 4, 7, 9
neglect of research by, 67
public image of, 16–17
Cost, of mobility policy, 57
Counseling, 64
"Crown prince" issue, 32–33

D

Decision-makers
communication of plans to employees by, 22
interviews of, 15–16, 77–79
on management development, 35
perspectives of, 9
positions held by, 4–5
on setbacks of candidates, 25
and visibility, 37
Decision-making. *See* Management selection.
Depression babies, 16
Developing Managerial Competence: Changing Concepts, Emerging Practices, 67n
Dunnette, M. D., 2n, 53n, 67, 67n

E

Economic growth, management selection and, 57
Education
attitude of chief executive toward, 2
and management development, 11, 51–52
and management selection, 71
motivational implications of, 50–51
for upper management, 11
See also Special education.
Executives
assigned outside of United States, 39
mature, 2
See also Decision-makers; Intermediate managers; Junior management; Middle management; Senior executives.
Executive talent. *See* Talent.
Experience, promotees' opinions on, 76–77

F

Favoritism, 11, 46
Fiedler, F. E., 36n
Fleishman, Edwin A., 6n
Foreign assignments, 58

Formal training. *See* Education.
"Frontiers in Group Dynamics: Concept, Method and Reality in Social Science," 57

G

"Gate-opening" positions, 38
Glickman, Albert S., 6*n*
Godfrey, E. P., 36*n*
Government, management selection in, 80–82
Great Depression, 8
Growth rates, management development criteria and, 73–74

H

Hahn, Clifford P., 6*n*
Holl, D. M., 36*n*
"Hot prospect" files, 82
Human Relations, 57
Human resources allocation, 1
Human Resources Research Program, 6*n*

I

Industrial Management Review, 2*n*
Innovation, rate of advance and, 24
Institute for Research on Organizational Behavior, 6*n*

Intelligence, management selection and, 71
Intermediate managers
selection of, 13–14
succession of, 9
Interpersonal Competence and Organizational Effectiveness, 59*n*
Interviewees
attitude toward specialization, 51–52
on corporate staff jobs, 41
and counseling, 64
on formal education, 48
on job descriptions, 23
See also Decision-makers; Promotees.
Interviewers, 6, 6*n*
Interviews
questions asked, 6, 76–79
selection of subjects for, 4–5
strategy of, 6

J

Job descriptions
changes in, 15, 27–28
and management selection, 12–13
and man-in-job concept, 10, 22–24
and personnel mix, 55
promotees' opinions on, 76
and visibility factor, 38–39

Job performance. *See* Performance; Performance rating.
Junior management, performance rating of, 20–21

L

Lawler, E. E., 2n, 53
Leabo, D. A., 2n
Levy, Seymour, 67, 67n
Lewin, K., 57n
Line-staff priority, 41–42

M

Man-in-job concept, 10, 22–24
Man in Management Award Dinner, 17n
Management
    of executive development program, 62–65
    psychological testing of, 39
    See also Decision-makers; Executives; Intermediate managers; Junior management; Middle management.
Management development
    and age, 10
    American Institutes for Research study of
        method used for, 3–6
        perspective of, 7–9
        purpose of, 2–3
        selection of corporations and subjects for, 4

    strategy of interviewing used in, 6
    articles on, 2
    and changes in nature of business, 53
    in company divisions, 30
    defining research issues for, 66–68
    and favoritism, 11
    and formal education, 2
    and moving to another company, 27
    organization policy for, 52–53
    and rate of advance, 24–26
    and testing, 10-11
    top level support and involvement in, 9–11, 60–61
    and personnel department, 62
    research assumptions, 68–70
    research plan for, 70–75
    and special education, 47–50
    training programs for, 11
    See also Management development programs; Management selection; Succession.
"Management Development as a Process of Influence," 2n
Management development programs, 30, 35
    approach of personnel and training experts to, 8
    cooperative, 31
    design of personnel flow through, 54–55
    determining, 52–53
    evaluations of, 64
    managers of, 60, 62–65
    in survey companies, 9

at upper and lower echelons, 34
Management development systems. *See* Management development programs.
Management Effectiveness, 2n
Management selection
and accidental versus planned discovery, 38–40
and accomplishment versus development objectives, 32
and communication to selected promotees, 22
comparative analysis of, 72–73
and competition among candidates, 16
and criteria for effective performance, 53
and "crown prince" issue, 32–33
and demand for personnel under certain managers, 30–31
and determination of characteristics of promotees, 36, 70–73
and education, 48–49
emotional factors in, 58–60
and employee participation in conferences, 39
and general and specific development programs compared, 34–36
by government and universities, 80–82
group methods of, 19–21
and "hot prospect" files, 82
and image of big business, 16–17

and individual and organization stress, 26–27
and informal comparisons, 18
and job control, 23–24
job-description, people-description method of, 12–13
and large versus small division benefits, 31
methods of, 13–16, 19–22
and mobility, 57–58
and outside recruitment, 46
and performance rating, 20–22
and personnel flow and mix, 54–55
and problem situations, 43
and raiding of divisions, 31
and rate of advance, 28–29
and self-effacement, 44–45
and setbacks, 25
and situational - organizational variables, 27–28
small business context of, 13
and specialization, 51–52
and stability versus change, 55–57
and supply and demand, 16–17
timing and sequence of, 17–19
and visibility, 34–38, 40–46
See also Succession.
Michigan Business Reports, 2n
Middle management
and computerization, 17
rotation of, 57
selection of top-management from, 29
Military service, shortage of top management personnel and, 16

"Misplaced modesty," 44–45
Mobility, management selection
and, 57–58

N

"New look" principle, 42–44
New product development, management selection and, 72
Nonconformity, rate of advance and, 24
Nonprofit organizations, management selection in, 81
Nonvisible assignments, 39

O

Organization charts, 28
Organizational Psychology, 47n
Outside recruitment, 17, 27, 46

P

Pace College, Advisory Council of, 17n
Performance
   criteria form, 53
   and education, 48–49
   in educational situations, 50
   ineffective, 59
   and management selection, 45, 48
   and mobility, 58

See also Performance rating.
Performance rating, 20–22
   and man-in-job description, 22–24
   and management selection, 71
   See also Performance.
Personality factors
   in management selection, 54–55, 58–60, 70–73
   and managers of development programs, 62–65
   and special education, 47
Personnel departments, role in management training and selection, 62
Personnel flow and mix, 54–55
Personnel Psychology, 67n
Pillsbury Company, 67
Predictions of ultimate level of executive, 21
Preparation for Business Leadership: Views of Top Executives, 2, 2n
Professional associations, 41, 81
Promotees
   attitudes toward formal training, 50–51
   interviews, 76–77
   and knowledge of promotion, 22
   perspectives of, 9
   positions held by, 4–5
   rate of advance of, 24–26
   reaction to being chosen, 28
   reasons for promotion, 44
   recognition of, 14
   and visibility, 37

Promotion. *See* Management selection; Succession.
Psychological factors. *See* Personality factors.

R

Raiding, 31
Reaction, to newly selected manager, of customers, employees, financiers, investors, unions, 15–16
Richardson Foundation, 2n, 67

S

Salary, management selection and, 71
Schein, Edgar H., 2, 2n, 47n, 75
Self-confidence, 51
Senior executives
  background of, 8
  interview procedures, 3
  and management development and succession, 35–36
  See also Decision-makers; Executives.
Situational-organizational variables, 27–28
Social values
  and formal training, 50–51
  and organizational effectiveness, 48
Special education, 47–50. *See also* Education.

Specialization, 43
  and college education, 51–52
Staff positions, 41–42
Statistical comparisons of management development systems, 69
Stress
  and career advancement, 26–27
  of management selection, 59
Studies in Personnel Policy, 67n
Subsidiaries
  candidates from 39
  vice-presidential appointments to, 18
Succession
  and failure of previous employee, 43
  and personnel flow and mix, 54–55
  presidential, 18
  role of senior executive in, 35
  of top and intermediate managers compared, 9–10
  See also Management development; Management selection.
Supply and demand, 16–17
Swinyard, A. W., 2n

T

Talent
  hidden, 82
  identification of, 36
  shortage of, 9, 16–17

Talent pools
  elimination from, 26
  in small divisions, 31
Technical achievement, promotion
    and, 51–52
Technical homogeneity, 55
Testing, 10–11, 34
Time factor
  and management development
    research, 69
  and top management selection,
    17–19
Top management. *See* Decision-
    makers; Executives; Senior
    executives.
Training. *See* Education; Manage-
    ment development.
Turnover forecasts, 54

U

Universities, management selec-
    tion in, 81

V

Veto, 19
Visibility, 34–36
  and "gate-opening" positions,
    38
  improvement of, 40–46
  provision for, 39

W

Watson, Thomas J., Jr., 17*n*
Weick, K. E., 2*n*
Wikstron, W. S., 67*n*
World War II, 8

OTHER SUPPLEMENTARY PAPERS PUBLISHED BY CED

To order CED publications please indicate number in column entitled "# Copies Desired." Then mail this order form and check for total amount in envelope to Distribution Division, CED, 477 Madison Ave., New York, 10022.

Order Number   **Copies Desired**

1S .. THE ECONOMICS OF A FREE SOCIETY
William Benton
October, 1944, 20 pages. (20¢)   _____

6S .. THE CHANGING ECONOMIC FUNCTION
OF THE CENTRAL CITY
Raymond Vernon
January, 1959, 92 pages, 14 tables, 8 charts. ($1.25)   _____

7S .. METROPOLIS AGAINST ITSELF
Robert C. Wood
March, 1959, 56 pages. ($1.00)   _____

10S .. DEVELOPING THE "LITTLE" ECONOMIES
Donald R. Gilmore
April, 1960, 160 pages, 20 tables. ($2.00)   _____

11S .. THE EDUCATION OF BUSINESSMEN
Leonard S. Silk
December, 1960, 48 pages, 9 tables. (75¢)   _____

13S .. THE SOURCES OF ECONOMIC GROWTH
IN THE UNITED STATES AND THE ALTERNATIVES BEFORE US
Edward F. Denison
January, 1962, 308 pages, 4 charts, 33 tables. ($4.00)   _____

15S .. FARMING, FARMERS, AND MARKETS
FOR FARM GOODS
Karl A. Fox, Vernon W. Ruttan, Lawrence W. Witt
November, 1962, 190 pages, 16 charts, 46 tables. ($3.00)   _____

16S .. THE COMMUNITY ECONOMIC BASE STUDY
Charles M. Tiebout
December, 1962, 98 pages, 6 charts, 12 tables. ($1.50)   _____

17S .. HOW A REGION GROWS—
AREA DEVELOPMENT IN THE U.S. ECONOMY
Harvey S. Perloff, with Vera W. Dodds
*March, 1963, 152 pages, 21 charts, 23 tables. ($2.25)**   _____

18S .. COMMUNITY ECONOMIC DEVELOPMENT EFFORTS:
FIVE CASE STUDIES
W. Paul Brann, V. C. Crisafulli, Donald R. Gilmore,
Jacob J. Kaufman, Halsey R. Jones, Jr., J. W. Milliman,
John H. Nixon, W. G. Pinnell
*December, 1964, 352 pages, 47 tables, 14 charts. ($2.75)**   _____

SEE OTHER SIDE→

19S .. CRISIS IN WORLD COMMUNISM—
MARXISM IN SEARCH OF EFFICIENCY
Frank O'Brien
January, 1965, 192 pages. ($2.75)*
_____

20S .. MEN NEAR THE TOP:
FILLING KEY POSTS IN THE FEDERAL SERVICE
John J. Corson and R. Shale Paul
April, 1966, 192 pages. ($3.00)*
_____

21S .. ECONOMIC DEVELOPMENT ISSUES:
LATIN AMERICA
Roberto Alemann (Argentina); Mario Henrique Simonsen
(Brazil); Sergio Undurraga Saavedra (Chile); Hernan
Echavarria (Colombia); Gustavo Romero Kolbeck
(Mexico); Romulo A. Ferrero (Peru).
August, 1967, 356 pages, 74 tables. ($4.25)*
_____

22S .. REGIONAL INTEGRATION AND
THE TRADE OF LATIN AMERICA
Roy Blough and Jack N. Behrman; Rómulo A. Ferrero
January, 1968, 184 pages, 14 tables. ($2.50)
_____

23S .. FISCAL ISSUES IN THE FUTURE OF FEDERALISM
Metropolitan Case Studies; The Potential Impact of General
Aid in Four Selected States; The Outlook for State and Local
Finance.
May, 1968, 288 pages, 56 tables. ($3.00)
_____

24S .. REMAKING THE INTERNATIONAL MONETARY SYSTEM: THE
RIO AGREEMENT AND BEYOND
Fritz Machlup
June, 1968, 176 pages, 2 tables. ($3.00)*
_____

25S .. ECONOMIC DEVELOPMENT ISSUES: GREECE,
ISRAEL, TAIWAN, THAILAND
Diomedes D. Psilos (Greece); Nadav Halevi (Israel); Shigeto
Kawano (Taiwan); Katsumi Mitani (Thailand)
July, 1968, 232 pages, 49 tables. ($4.00)*
_____

26S .. WHO ARE THE URBAN POOR?
Anthony Downs
October, 1968, 76 pages, 18 tables. ($1.00)
_____

27S .. TOP MANAGEMENT DEVELOPMENT AND SUCCESSION
An exploratory study by Albert S. Glickman, Clifford P.
Hahn, Edwin A. Fleishman, Brent Baxter of American Institutes for Research
November, 1968, 108 pages. ($2.00)*
_____

☐ Please bill me. (Remittance requested for orders under $3.00)
☐ Please send me CED's current publications list.
☐ I should like to know how I might receive all of CED's future publications
by becoming a Participant in the CED Reader-Forum.
* Hard cover edition available. Prices on request.